WWE

BEYOND
EXTreME

WRITTEN BY
DEAN MILLER

cOntents

EXTREME WARNING!

WWE SUPERSTARS ARE PROFESSIONAL ATHLETES. DON'T TRY THEIR MOVES AT HOME!

ePic entrances

Almost every Superstar enters the arena to fireworks and pounding rock music—but some take things to extremes, just to get under an opponent's skin and into their head!

One man army—flanked by two rows of Cena doppelgangers at *WrestleMania XXV*, John Cena sprints to the ring.

Cereal winners—The New Day emerge from a giant box of their Booty-O's cereal ("Made with 100% positivity!") at *WrestleMania 32*.

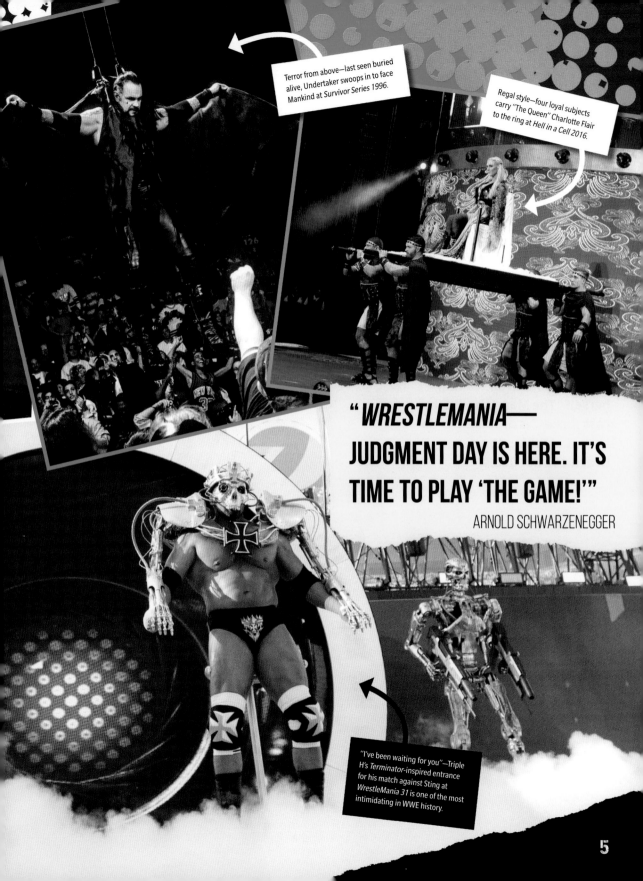

Terror from above—last seen buried alive, Undertaker swoops in to face Mankind at *Survivor Series 1996*.

Regal style—four loyal subjects carry "The Queen" Charlotte Flair to the ring at *Hell in a Cell 2016*.

"*WRESTLEMANIA*— JUDGMENT DAY IS HERE. IT'S TIME TO PLAY 'THE GAME!'"

ARNOLD SCHWARZENEGGER

"I've been waiting for you"—Triple H's *Terminator*-inspired entrance for his match against Sting at *WrestleMania 31* is one of the most intimidating in WWE history.

BECKY LYNCH

Since her NXT debut in 2014, Becky Lynch has been one of the WWE Universe's favorite Superstars. The fans seem willing to forgive and forget the most outrageously villainous behavior. Calling herself "The Man," the "Irish Lass Kicker" is prepared to do almost anything to anyone to achieve her goals.

"AT *WRESTLEMANIA*, WHEN ALL WAS SAID AND DONE, THIS WOMAN WHO WALKED IN WITH NOTHING, LEFT WITH <u>EVERYTHING!</u>"

BECKY LYNCH

First draft champ

During the 2016 WWE Draft, Becky Lynch was the first woman selected by *SmackDown*. She proved herself worthy of the honor at *Backlash* when she competed in a Six-Pack Elimination Match to crown the first-ever *SmackDown* Women's Champion. After outlasting Alexa Bliss, Naomi, Natalya, and Nikki Bella, Becky forced Carmella to submit to her excruciating Dis-arm-her move for the win.

Social media attacks

In the leadup to her Triple Threat Match for both the *RAW* and *SmackDown* Women's Championships in the main event of *WrestleMania 35*, Becky utilized a new weapon to get under the skins of rivals Ronda Rousey and Charlotte Flair—Twitter. Becky's posts mocked Rousey in particular, and from Ronda's angry reactions, Becky's plan worked. The tweets and clever Photoshops delighted the WWE Universe and got Lynch mainstream press, leading into her historic *WrestleMania* victory.

All or nothing

One of the main events of the first-ever all-women's pay-per-view *Evolution* featured Becky Lynch defending her *SmackDown* Women's Championship in a Last Woman Standing Match against Charlotte Flair. The two former best friends brutally assaulted each other, using tables, ladders, and chairs. Powerbombing Flair from the top rope through a table, Becky retained her championship.

FaNtastic Feats

"Two for the show"—John Cena looks to end his Triple Threat Match by lifting Edge and Big Show on his shoulders for an Attitude Adjustment.

"MY MOUTH WAS AGAPE WHEN I SAW JOHN CENA LIFT BOTH BIG SHOW AND EDGE SIMULTANEOUSLY!"

JERRY "THE KING" LAWLER

Some of the world's most powerful athletes compete in WWE, and the WWE Universe is used to seeing them demonstrate impressive strength. But every once in a while, a Superstar pulls off a feat of strength so incredible that it leaves fans open-mouthed ...

Pulling power—living up to his "World's Strongest Man" moniker, Mark Henry tows a tractor trailer across the finish line.

Heavy lifting—Beth Phoenix delivers a backbreaker to both Mickie James and Melina at Judgment Day 2008.

Heard around the world—Hulk Hogan scoops up the mighty Andre the Giant and body slams him to the mat at WrestleMania III.

Big push—sending a message to his WrestleMania 21 Sumo Match opponent Akebono, Big Show flips over a massive Jeep.

9

SWANTON BOMB BLAST!

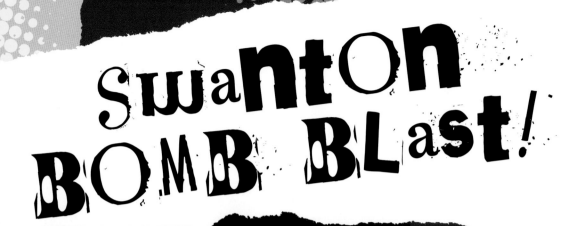

The Hardys, Dudleys, and Edge & Christian were competing in the first-ever Triangle Ladder Match at *WrestleMania 2000*. Showing a blatant disregard for his own health, Jeff Hardy decided to take Bubba Ray Dudley out of the match ....

High stakes

All six men were more than willing to put their bodies on the line to become World Tag Team Champions. But Jeff Hardy took things to the next level. Climbing to the top of a massive ladder, he nailed Bubba Ray with a death-defying Swanton Bomb. The impact sent Bubba Ray crashing through a table. While the move put Bubba Ray out of the match, it also knocked out Jeff, allowing Edge & Christian to win!

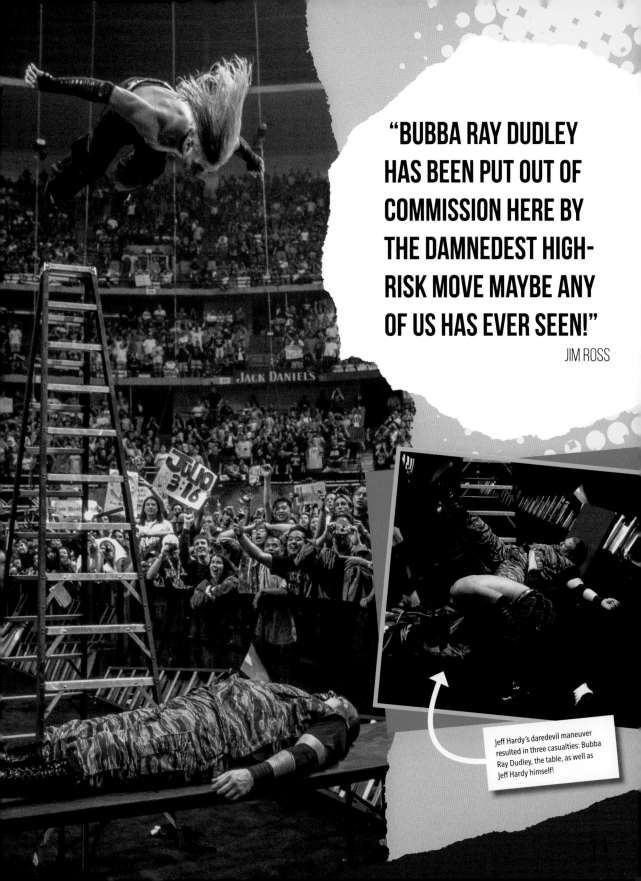

"BUBBA RAY DUDLEY HAS BEEN PUT OUT OF COMMISSION HERE BY THE DAMNEDEST HIGH-RISK MOVE MAYBE ANY OF US HAS EVER SEEN!"

JIM ROSS

Jeff Hardy's daredevil maneuver resulted in three casualties: Bubba Ray Dudley, the table, as well as Jeff Hardy himself!

HELL IN A CELL

Originally designed to prevent any outside interference in a match, this demonic structure has brought untold pain to the men and women battling within. Anything goes, and careers have been altered—even ended—by Hell in a Cell's unforgiving steel.

"WHAT A WRETCHED ENVIRONMENT!"

JIM ROSS

A monster debut

The first-ever Hell in a Cell, between Shawn Michaels and Undertaker, was a Number One Contenders bout, with the winner set to face Bret "Hit Man" Hart at *Survivor Series 1997*. Undertaker thought he could easily deal with Michaels without Michaels' D-Generation X brethren to help him. Undertaker got the shock of his life when his younger brother Kane, making his WWE debut, entered the cell and Tombstoned Undertaker—giving Michaels an easy win.

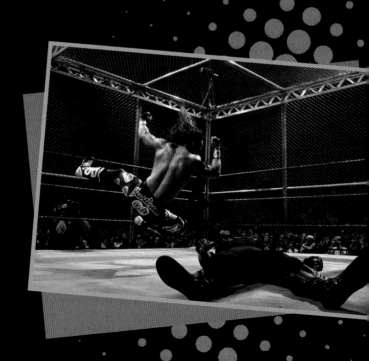

Armageddon outta here!

Commissioner Mick Foley was a certified expert on Hell in a Cell, having participated in four of the first six matches in history. So when five men—Undertaker, Triple H, The Rock, Stone Cold Steve Austin, and Rikishi felt they had a claim to Kurt Angle's WWE Championship, he had a unique solution—a six-man Hell in a Cell. All the participants were soon bloodied and battered, and, at one point, Undertaker threw Rikishi off the cell onto a truck bed parked next to it. Amid the chaos and mayhem, Angle managed to steal a pinfall on The Rock to win and retain his title.

Extreme weapons inside the cell

Some Superstars don't think the cell is enough to punish their opponents, so they take advantage of the match's no-disqualification stipulation to employ some very cruel and unusual weapons ...

Fire alarm—Cactus Jack threatens Triple H with a flaming 2x4 at *No Way Out 2000*.

Watch the birdie—Edge assaults Undertaker with a camera at *Survivor Series 2007*.

Sharp practice—Batista wields a steel chair wrapped in barbed wire at *Vengeance 2005*.

Charlotte doesn't hold back

The thirty-fifth Hell in a Cell Match, held at *Hell in a Cell 2016*, was a historic event, as it featured two women competing in *Hell in a Cell* for the first time. Charlotte and Sasha Banks fought with reckless abandon both inside and outside the cell. Chairs and tables were employed and Charlotte was eventually able to keep Banks down for a three count, allowing her to become *RAW* Women's Champion for the third time in her career.

Burning Down the House

Bray Wyatt believed that Randy Orton was a devoted member of his villainous Wyatt Family, but Bray Wyatt was in for a mighty shock. The Superstar known as "The Viper" was running a long con.

Orton admires his handiwork as the Wyatt compound burns.

"Don't do this!"—Bray Wyatt sobs as Orton sets his power base on fire and consigns "the soul of Sister Abigail" to "eternal damnation."

"ONCE YOU JOIN 'EM, AND IT'S THE RIGHT TIME, SCREW 'EM!"

RANDY ORTON

Orton poses with Sister Abigail's rocking chair as he prepares to torch Bray Wyatt's compound—"A place where you can smell the stench of evil in the air."

"The Viper" strikes

The WWE Universe was shocked that Randy Orton had decided to live by the old adage "If you can't beat 'em, join 'em," pledging loyalty to Bray Wyatt and joining his cultlike Wyatt Family. Orton claimed that he would not challenge Wyatt for his WWE Championship at *WrestleMania 33*, even though it was his right as the winner of the 2017 *Royal Rumble*. However, Orton was just looking to destroy Wyatt from the inside. While a confident Wyatt was addressing the WWE Universe during a *SmackDown* episode on February 28, 2017, Orton showed up at the Wyatt compound, the center of Bray Wyatt's power, and set it ablaze!

eLiMiNatiOn cHaMBer

Who's next?—Braun Strowman scores another pin in his record-setting performance.

Who's next?—Braun Strowman scores another pin in his record-setting performance.

Ten tons of steel. Two miles of chain. The Elimination Chamber is specifically designed to test a Superstar's mettle. To win, you have to outlast five other competitors, and with steel surrounding the ring and no escape possible, that's a tall order!

Five eliminations, no victory

One of the most dominant performances in Elimination Chamber history occurred in 2018, when Braun Strowman eliminated five other competitors. At most Elimination Chamber Matches, that would be a clean sweep for the win. Unfortunately for Strowman, for the first time ever, six other men competed in the match. While "The Monster Among Men" took out Seth Rollins, Finn Bálor, Elias, The Miz, and John Cena, Roman Reigns proved one Superstar too many and pinned him to win.

"RIGHT NOW, I'VE GOT A FIRST-CLASS TICKET TO HELL, AND I WONDER WHO'S COMING WITH ME?"

Extra hurt—the most brutal Extreme Chamber combatants use the chain-link walls to inflict even more punishment.

An extreme twist

At 2006's *December to Dismember*, ECW upped the Elimination Chamber ante, putting weapons in each pod for their Extreme Elimination Chamber. Bobby Lashley overcame five other men—plus a chair, table, crowbar, and barbed-wire baseball bat—to win the ECW Title for the first time in his career.

A first for the chamber

The inaugural winners of the Women's Tag Team Championship were settled at *Elimination Chamber 2019*. Despite being one of the first two teams in the chamber, the Boss 'n' Hug Connection (Sasha Banks and Bayley) outlasted five other teams to capture the titles.

Mighty crowded

Occasionally, Elimination Chamber pods are used to stagger Superstars' entry into a match. The pods can barely contain some of the larger competitors, so it was a particularly tight squeeze when all three members of The New Day ended up in the same pod.

UNDERTAKER

For almost three decades, the sinister spirit of Undertaker has ruled WWE. Whenever rival Superstars think he could be gone for good, a tolling bell announces the spooky return of "The Deadman." Undertaker has held the World Championship seven times, but it often seems as if he's more interested in claiming his opponents' souls ...

> **"I DON'T MAKE MISTAKES. I BURY THEM."**
>
> UNDERTAKER

A hellish comeback

Kane's latest betrayal of his sibling Undertaker had left "The Deadman" in a vegetative state for most of the summer of 2010. Kane exploited his brother's absence to capture the World Heavyweight Championship and to terrorize the *SmackDown* roster. However, Undertaker arose once again and began playing scary mind games with his demonic brother, emerging through the ring during a match and dragging Kane down to hell!

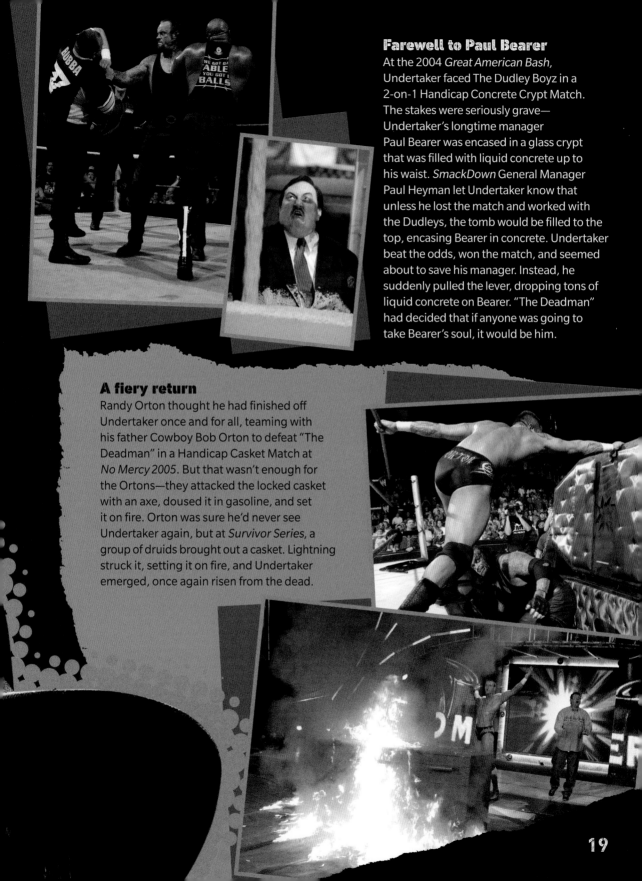

Farewell to Paul Bearer

At the 2004 *Great American Bash*, Undertaker faced The Dudley Boyz in a 2-on-1 Handicap Concrete Crypt Match. The stakes were seriously grave— Undertaker's longtime manager Paul Bearer was encased in a glass crypt that was filled with liquid concrete up to his waist. *SmackDown* General Manager Paul Heyman let Undertaker know that unless he lost the match and worked with the Dudleys, the tomb would be filled to the top, encasing Bearer in concrete. Undertaker beat the odds, won the match, and seemed about to save his manager. Instead, he suddenly pulled the lever, dropping tons of liquid concrete on Bearer. "The Deadman" had decided that if anyone was going to take Bearer's soul, it would be him.

A fiery return

Randy Orton thought he had finished off Undertaker once and for all, teaming with his father Cowboy Bob Orton to defeat "The Deadman" in a Handicap Casket Match at *No Mercy 2005*. But that wasn't enough for the Ortons—they attacked the locked casket with an axe, doused it in gasoline, and set it on fire. Orton was sure he'd never see Undertaker again, but at *Survivor Series*, a group of druids brought out a casket. Lightning struck it, setting it on fire, and Undertaker emerged, once again risen from the dead.

Jake the Snake strikes

Jake "The Snake" Roberts was known for bringing his pet Damian—an enormous python—to the ring. One day, however, he decided to deploy an even more dangerous snake …

Biting back

After losing his retirement match against The Ultimate Warrior at *WrestleMania VII*, Randy "Macho Man" Savage had embraced a new career as a television commentator. But Jake "The Snake" Roberts kept poking the bear, harassing the "Macho Man" and questioning his manhood. Savage finally went to confront Roberts in the ring, but "The Snake" got the better of the confrontation and tied Savage up in the ropes. He then horrified the WWE Universe by producing a massive king cobra and letting it sink its teeth into the bicep of the "Macho Man."

"I DON'T THINK THAT SNAKE'S BEEN DEVENOMIZED!"

WWE CHAIRMAN MR. MCMAHON

21

A battle with Undertaker is always a risky business, but Mankind could not have imagined how much he was putting on the line by entering this match. Not one for taking pity, Undertaker unleashed his full aggression on Mankind and took things to a whole new level.

A TUMBLE THROUGH HELL

Undertaker surveys the havoc he has caused after tossing Mankind off the top of the cage.

20 FT

Thrown off the cage

Rather than start Hell in a Cell inside the ring, Mankind climbed to the top of the cage, daring Undertaker to do the same. That was Mankind's first mistake. They battled briefly on top of the 20-foot-high (6.1-m-high) cell, before Undertaker threw Mankind off it, sending him crashing right through the announcers' table. It seemed like the match was over, as medical personnel started wheeling Mankind out on a gurney.

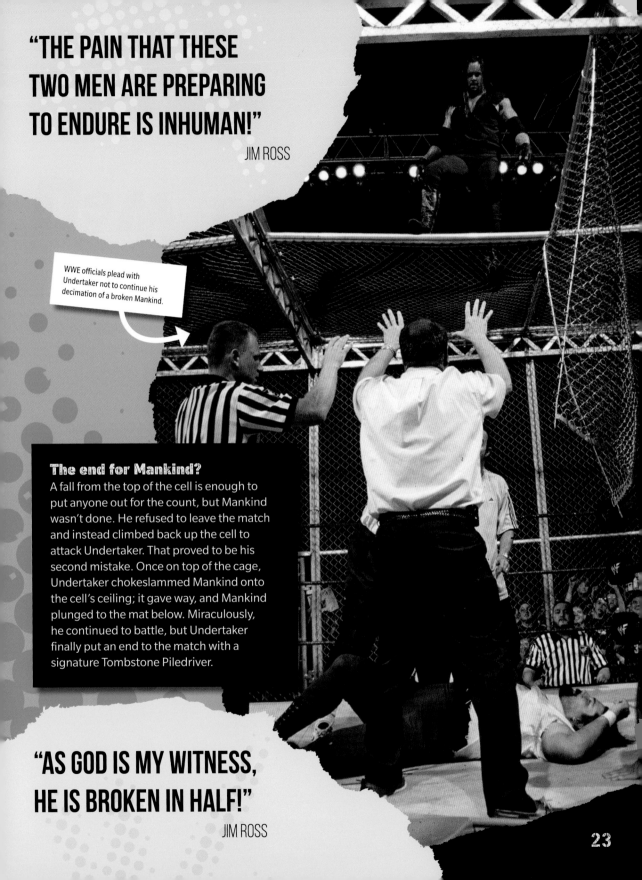

"THE PAIN THAT THESE TWO MEN ARE PREPARING TO ENDURE IS INHUMAN!"

JIM ROSS

WWE officials plead with Undertaker not to continue his decimation of a broken Mankind.

The end for Mankind?

A fall from the top of the cell is enough to put anyone out for the count, but Mankind wasn't done. He refused to leave the match and instead climbed back up the cell to attack Undertaker. That proved to be his second mistake. Once on top of the cage, Undertaker chokeslammed Mankind onto the cell's ceiling; it gave way, and Mankind plunged to the mat below. Miraculously, he continued to battle, but Undertaker finally put an end to the match with a signature Tombstone Piledriver.

"AS GOD IS MY WITNESS, HE IS BROKEN IN HALF!"

JIM ROSS

A wild Street Fight between Kurt Angle and Shane McMahon led to a series of suplexes that turned Shane into something like a human wrecking ball!

DeMOLitiON MeN

Fighting for WCW

After he purchased WCW from under his father Vince's nose, Shane McMahon targeted WWE and its Superstars, particularly former Gold Medalist Kurt Angle. Out for revenge, Angle challenged McMahon to a Street Fight at 2001's *King of the Ring*, and the brawl continued to the top of the stage. Angle slammed McMahon into the set wall with an overhead belly-to-belly suplex.

Guided missile—Kurt Angle bounces Shane McMahon off the *King of the Ring* set.

> ## "THESE MEN ARE LITERALLY BEATING THE HELL, THE BLOOD, AND THE PULP OUT OF EACH OTHER!"
>
> JIM ROSS

A second overhead belly-to-belly suplex shatters the set wall, sending Shane crashing through it.

Glutton for punishment
Angle was not done with McMahon, and he suplexed him through two glass walls before tossing him head first through another. Angle then dragged a dazed Shane back to the ring. Amazingly, McMahon still offered some resistance, but Angle smacked him with a piece of lumber and pinned him after a top-rope Angle Slam.

T#ree Stages Of HeLL

Either deep-seated loathing or an insatiable desire to inflict pain draws Superstars into a Three Stages of Hell Match. Having to win two out of three specialty matches is so grueling that this match has only happened four times.

Heavyweight hell

Friends turned bitter enemies Triple H and Shawn Michaels met in a Three Stages of Hell Match for the World Heavyweight Championship at *Armageddon 2002*. Triple H won the Street Fight, despite Michaels nailing him with a flaming 2x4 wrapped in barbed wire. Michaels then put "The Game" through a table to win the Steel Cage Match, but Triple H won the Ladder Match to regain the title.

Brutal blows

The animosity between Triple H and Stone Cold Steve Austin had risen since, in his desire to become WWE Champion, Triple H had arranged for Austin to be hit by a car. On Austin's return, a 2 Falls Out of 3 Match was set at *No Way Out 2001*. In the final and most vicious match, Triple H claimed his second and final fall when he pinned Austin after the two hit each other with a sledgehammer and a 2x4 wrapped in barbed wire.

The Viper bites back

At *The Bash 2009*, Triple H might have stayed undefeated in Three Stages of Hell Matches if not for Randy Orton's Legacy allies. Orton won the first match by disqualification, but "The Game" evened things up by winning the Street Fights. However, the deciding Stretcher Match was not a fair contest, as Cody Rhodes and Ted DiBiase helped Orton completely overwhelm Triple H.

Payback time

At *Payback 2013*, John Cena defended the WWE Title against Ryback. The bout featured three match types never before seen in a Three Stages of Hell Match: a Lumberjack Match, a Tables Match, and an Ambulance Match, in which one Superstar has to get the other into an ambulance. In a ring surrounded by Lumberjacks, Ryback pinned Cena to take the first fall. Cena put Ryback through a table to grab the second fall, but Ryback then put Cena through the announce table. Cena looked in trouble as Ryback hauled him toward the ambulance, but recovered, smacked Ryback with parts of the vehicle, and finally sent him crashing through the ambulance's roof to win.

> ## "I'M WALKING INTO HELL, BUT I'M WALKING OUT SAYING: 'THE CHAMP IS HERE!'"
>
> JOHN CENA

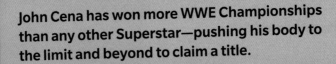

John Cena has won more WWE Championships than any other Superstar—pushing his body to the limit and beyond to claim a title.

JOHN CeNa's 16 WORLD TiTLes

Edging out Edge

John Cena's 2006 rivalry with Edge was one of the most compelling in his career. It seemed unlikely that he'd defeat "The Rated-R Superstar" for the title at *Unforgiven*, as it was taking place in Edge's hometown (Toronto) and was a match type that Edge specialized in (TLC). But Cena proved a quick study in his first TLC match, sending Edge crashing through a stack of tables from a ladder to grab the championship for the third time.

Eliminating the Competition

2010's *Elimination Chamber* featured six men competing in the fearsome chamber for the WWE Championship. Cena faced long odds, being trapped in the structure with longtime rivals Triple H and Randy Orton, as well as current champion Sheamus and two others. Yet Cena outlasted the competition in this grueling match, finally forcing Triple H to submit to his STF maneuver to capture the WWE Championship once again!

Extreme Steel Cage

The main event of *Extreme Rules 2011* saw The Miz defending the WWE Championship against his former tag team partner John Morrison and John Cena. Once again, the odds were stacked against Cena, as he was often the target of The Miz's brutality and Morrison's innovative offense. An Attitude Adjustment from the top rope allowed Cena to gain a pinfall victory on The Miz, making him WWE Champion for the eighth time in his career.

Championship Money

The Money in the Bank Match at 2014's *Money in the Bank* was supposed to award a title opportunity for the WWE World Heavyweight Championship. But injury had forced reigning champ Daniel Bryan to vacate the title, so the match became a championship bout. Eight men, seven past and future champions among them, battled to be the first to climb the ladder and seize the championship. John Cena's Attitude Adjustment dropped Randy Orton onto Kane, whom he'd also nailed with an Attitude Adjustment. With his foes stacked like firewood, Cena retrieved the title to win the match.

CHYNA

A true trailblazer in the "Women's Evolution" in WWE, Chyna took on all comers, battling both women and men. After debuting as a bodyguard for Triple H, Chyna became the first woman to hold the Intercontinental Championship and the first woman to compete in the men's *Royal Rumble*.

Female power

When Chyna joined WWE in 1997, women often managed male Superstars, but did not get involved in physical battles. But Chyna had no problem defending her employer, Triple H. Before long, Chyna became an enforcer for the D-Generation X faction, intimidating all with her impressive bodybuilder physique and fierce attitude.

Chyna cleans house

Intercontinental Champion Jeff Jarrett was not happy that Chyna was the Number One Contender for his title. Mocking her, he claimed a woman's place was in the kitchen and agreed to face her in a Good Housekeeping Match, where opponents attack each other with houshold appliances and food. Chyna showed him her place was in the ring and matched the sexist Jarrett blow for blow. After nailing him with his own guitar and covering him in flour, Chyna became the first female Intercontinental Champion.

The bigger they come ...

Not only did Chyna enter the 1999 *Royal Rumble*, she earned the coveted Number 30 spot by winning a warm-up match between the members of the Corporation. Mr. McMahon thought that he'd won the match, but Chyna rocked up and threw him out of the ring. Chyna performed an even more impressive feat at the Rumble, eliminating the "World's Strongest Man," Mark Henry, from the competition. Unfortunately, Stone Cold Steve Austin then tossed her out of the match.

Extreme punishment

Chyna held the Women's Championship once in her career. She earned the title at *WrestleMania X-Seven* in one of the most dominant championship challenges in history, taking out current champion Ivory in less than three minutes. Chyna could have pinned Ivory even sooner, but she lifted the champion off the mat before the three count just so she could dole out more punishment.

WILD, WILD WEDDINGS

Who doesn't love a good wedding? Unfortunately, when it comes to a WWE ceremony, all too often everything that can go wrong *will* go wrong—and then some!

UNHOLY MATRIMONY

A terrified Stephanie McMahon is strapped to Undertaker's symbol. "The Deadman" will make her his bride, unless Mr. McMahon gives him WWE.

Rescue comes in the form of Mr. McMahon's enemy Stone Cold Steve Austin, who cannnot watch such evil without taking action!

JILTED!

A blissfully happy Daniel Bryan and AJ Lee prepare to exchange marriage vows ...

AJ skips up the aisle after leaving Bryan flat for a more attractive proposition—the position of *RAW* General Manager!

UNLUCKY LITA

Matt Hardy's brave intervention is in vain. Kane disposes of him, and then, grinning all over his face, carries off Lita, his new bride.

When the groom is as demonic as Kane, it is only fitting that the bride wears black. "I hate you, Kane, more than life itself," says Lita.

Kane nails Matt Hardy—the man Lita says she truly loves—with a big boot when he tries to interrupt the bizarre proceedings.

... Kane appears, and, showing that hell hath no fury like "The Big Red Monster," destroys the wedding chapel and Tombstones the padre!

WRECKED!

Lita is seemingly free to marry again, with Edge the lucky man. But just before their love story can have a happy ending ...

BARE NECCESSITIES

To prove their love, Al and Dawn Marie decide to recite their vows in their underwear!

It's a true May and December wedding when Dawn Marie and Torrie Wilson's father Al prepare to tie the knot.

nxt invasion

NXT winner Wade Barrett led seven NXT rookies to the ring. Their goal: To take down WWE Superstars—starting with WWE Champion John Cena—and then caused chaos in the arena.

Even ringside personnel found themselves targets of the Nexus' brutal rampage.

Not only did they decimate John Cena, the octet of NXT rookies even tore apart the ring itself!

Next-level chaos

The June 10, 2010 episode of *RAW* was a viewers' choice episode, where the WWE Universe got to select John Cena's opponent for the night's main event. Cena and CM Punk were battling in a back-and-forth affair when Wade Barrett, winner of NXT Season 1, sauntered to the ring. But he wasn't alone; seven other NXT rookies emerged and the eight men, who would become known as the Nexus, wreaked absolute havoc. They attacked television announcers and WWE personnel, destroyed equipment, tore the ring apart, and mercilessly beat down Cena, who left the ring on a stretcher. This shocking display announced the arrival of a new and vicious faction in WWE.

eXtreMeLY S#OrT TitLe reigns

Selling Out

André the Giant faced Hulk Hogan in February 1988's *The Main Event*. Thanks to an evil twin referee (whom Ted DiBiase had secretly hired), Hogan lost the WWE Championship. But André didn't keep the title—he immediately surrendered it to the "Million Dollar Man" Ted DiBiase. Unfortunately for DiBiase, the title transfer was ruled invalid and the title was vacated, putting the length of André's highly contentious reign at just moments.

Every champ wants to hold their title for as long as they can, but sometimes titles are lost before the nameplate can even be changed on the championship!

Hulk Hogan protests that Yokozuna and Mr. Fuji cheated to defeat Bret Hart for the WWE Championship at *WrestleMania IX*.

"I'M NOT SURE IF ANDRÉ COULD JUST GIVE THE CHAMPIONSHIP AWAY ..."

JESSE "THE BODY" VENTURA

Too much, too soon

Yokozuna's crowning career achievement should have come at *WrestleMania IX*. He had just defeated WWE Champion Bret Hart in the last match of the night. But the new champ's manager, Mr. Fuji, challenged Hulk Hogan to a match then and there. Fuji tried to throw salt in Hogan's eyes, but Hogan dodged—and proceeded to defeat Yokozuna and win the WWE Championship in a mere 22 seconds.

Scramble for the title

In 2008, WWE introduced the Championship Scramble. Five Superstars compete in a 20-minute match and whoever scores the last pinfall or submission in the time is the winner. In the Championship Scramble Match at *Unforgiven 2008*, the title unofficially changed hands seven times. Brian Kendrick held it once and Jeff Hardy captured it three times, then MVP seemed the likely winner. However, his reign lasted barely any time at all: Triple H, who entered the match as title holder, gave MVP a Pedigree at the last moment, to leave the match still WWE Champion.

Chris Jericho pins Kane to steal a title victory as time runs out in the World Heavyweight Championship Scramble Match.

Melina pins Jillian Hall for the Divas Championship on the same night Hall had captured the title for the only time in her WWE career.

Randy Orton takes advantage of a Pedigreed Daniel Bryan to cash in his Money in the Bank opportunity and pin Bryan moments after he'd won the championship.

Bayley prematurely ends Charlotte Flair's *SmackDown* Women's Championship reign with a big elbow.

Smash and grab

The Money in the Bank Match was introduced at *WrestleMania 21*. Ever since, champions have had to watch out for briefcase holders cashing in their title opportunities at the worst possible moment. Opportunistic Superstars see a wounded, exhausted champion and strike. At *Money in the Bank 2019*, Charlotte outlasted Becky Lynch to win the *SmackDown* Women's Championship, but Bayley suddenly cashed in her opportunity to drop a top-rope elbow on Charlotte to win the title. Flair's reign had lasted less than a minute!

EDge's 31 CHaMPiONs#iPs

WWE Hall of Famer Edge won an astounding 31 different championships during his career. After making his name as a tag team specialist with Christian, Edge went on to win 17 singles championships, including 11 World Titles.

Edge & Christian win a grueling triangle ladder match for the World Tag Team Championship at *WrestleMania 2000*.

Edge also held the United States Championship once, outlasting Kurt Angle to grab the title in an impromptu match on *RAW* in December 2001.

Edge captures yet another Tag Team Championship, this time with childhood idol Hulk Hogan as his partner.

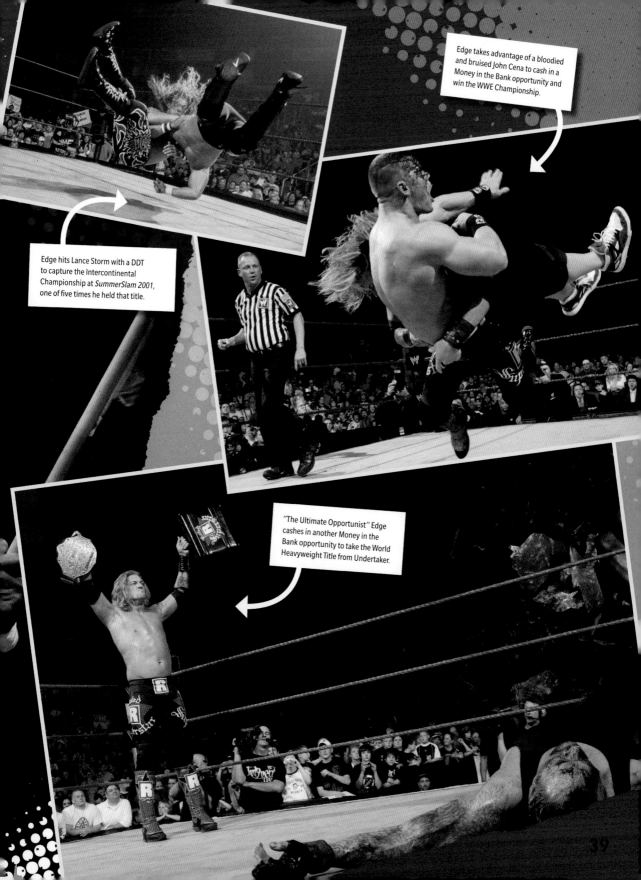

Edge takes advantage of a bloodied and bruised John Cena to cash in a Money in the Bank opportunity and win the WWE Championship.

Edge hits Lance Storm with a DDT to capture the Intercontinental Championship at *SummerSlam 2001*, one of five times he held that title.

"The Ultimate Opportunist" Edge cashes in another Money in the Bank opportunity to take the World Heavyweight Title from Undertaker.

iron strength

It's the ultimate test of physical and mental stamina. A quick pinfall or disqualification won't end an Iron Man Match—instead, Superstars battle for a set period of time, often as long as an hour.

Sudden-death triumph

Perhaps the most famous Iron Man Match in WWE occurred at *WrestleMania XII* between two of the most bitter rivals in WWE history: Shawn Michaels and Bret Hart. The two traded move for move and hold for hold for the 60 minutes of action, but neither recorded a decision. WWE President Gorilla Monsoon decided that the match had to have a winner, so he declared a sudden-death overtime period. Michaels caught Hart with a superkick two minutes later to pin the "Hit Man" and win the WWE Championship for the first time in his career.

"The Deadman" decides

In WWE's second Iron Man Match, Triple H challenged The Rock for the WWE Title. Triple H seemed to have the match in hand with a 5-3 lead with less than 10 minutes left. But The Rock Pedigreed Triple H on the announcers' table to gain a countout decision and then pinned him to tie the score with two minutes left. Suddenly, Undertaker emerged and attacked Triple H. The Rock was disqualified and Triple H gained the match 6-5 and the WWE Title.

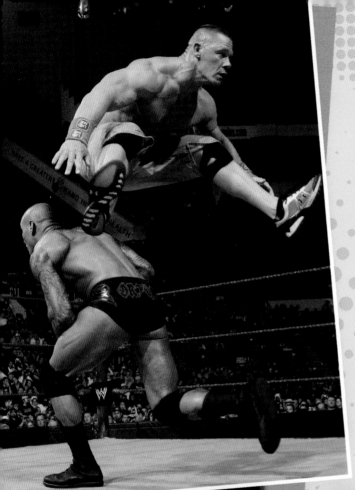

Iron women

The first Women's Iron Man Match occurred in NXT at *NXT Takeover: Respect 2015*. Bayley was the NXT Women's Champion, but previous title holder Sasha Banks felt her win was a fluke and was looking to take her title back. In the 30-minute match, Banks grabbed an early lead and was 2-1 up at the halfway point. Bayley pinned Banks and, as time was running out, it looked like the match was heading for a draw. With both Superstars on the point of exhaustion, Banks seized Bayley in her signature back-breaking Bank Statement finisher. With just seconds to go, Bayley broke the hold and got Banks to submit to a scissored arm bar, capturing the match and keeping her title.

Anything goes

When John Cena and Randy Orton competed in a 60-Minute Iron Man Match for the WWE Championship, they decided to up the ante by making it an Anything Goes Match as well. The added stipulation was a massive advantage for Orton, as it allowed his Legacy teammates Cody Rhodes and Ted DiBiase to interfere, helping Orton gain a pinfall decision. Kofi Kingston emerged with a steel chair to chase off Legacy, evening up the match. Finally, with the match tied at 5-all and seconds remaining, Cena locked Orton in his STF submission maneuver and forced him to submit, to win 6-5.

Hardy is famous for his face paint, explaining: "That's Jeff Hardy, the Charismatic Enigma, at his best."

JEFF HARDY

As one half of The Hardy Boyz as well as Team Xtreme, Jeff Hardy brought an aerial wizardry to WWE rings that has made him a beloved Superstar for decades.

New brood, new manager

Jeff and Matt Hardy briefly competed as the New Brood, battling the original Brood (Edge and Christian) in a best-of-five series of matches to earn the managerial services of Terri and $100,000. The deciding contest was at *No Mercy 1999*, WWE's first-ever tag team Ladder Match. With the money hanging above the ring, the four men battled so hard, it seemed that they'd be too exhausted to climb the ladder. But Jeff knocked Edge off a ladder and grabbed the cash, falling to the ring with his team's big score.

Jeff Hardy drives Christian into the mat while his brother sets up a ladder.

Uxtreme TLC

As one of The Hardy Boyz, Jeff Hardy helped invent the Tables, Ladders, and Chairs Match. So it seemed like an advantage for Jeff when he defended his World Heavyweight Championship against CM Punk in a TLC Match at *SummerSlam 2009*. But Punk, in his first-ever TLC Match, proved a quick study, forcing Hardy to execute some high-risk maneuvers. The most dangerous move of all was a Swanton Bomb off a massive ladder onto Punk on the announcers' desk, that rendered both men unconscious. They then somehow found the strength to battle for the title suspended above a ladder. A forearm smash from Punk sent Jeff tumbling, allowing Punk to claim the World Heavyweight Championship. A few moments later, Undertaker came to the ring and flattened the new champ.

Jeff Hardy flies off an 18-foot ladder, crashing through both CM Punk and the announcers' table!

Not missing a beat in his 2017 WWE return, Hardy tumbles through the air to put Cesaro through a ladder.

"OH MY GOD, I DON'T BELIEVE WHAT I JUST SAW!"

TODD GRISHAM, WITNESSING
A JEFF HARDY SWANTON BOMB

Team Xtreme returns

The WWE Universe had not seen The Hardy Boyz for almost eight years when they made a stunning return at *WrestleMania 33*, turning a Triple Threat Match for the *RAW* Tag Team Championship into a Fatal 4-Way. There was clearly no rust in their game as they overcame Sheamus & Cesaro, Gallows & Anderson, and Enzo & Big Cass to climb the ladder and win the titles. On the way, they used all their famous moves, such as Poetry in Motion—one Hardy springboards off the other to deliver a powerful kick—and Whisper in the Wind—Jeff throws himself backward off the top rope, twisting in the air and flattening his opponent.

THE MONTreaL ScreWJOB

One of the most infamous incidents in WWE History, the Montreal Screwjob led to a decade-long rift between WWE Chairman Mr. Vince McMahon and his own champion, Bret "Hit Man" Hart.

A new start

Things looked bleak for WWE. Longtime competitor Bret "Hit Man" Hart was set to leave and join the organization's bitter rival WCW. While it was not unusual for a Superstar to leave one company and join another, Bret was WWE Champion, and that complicated matters. WWE supremo Mr. McMahon did not want Hart to join WCW as the reigning WWE Champion, but Hart was doing everything possible to ensure he didn't lose the title to his most hated rival, Shawn Michaels. With the two set to meet at 1997's *Survivor Series*, something had to give.

McMahon plays dirty

Mr. McMahon was prepared to cheat to get his way. During the match, Michaels wrapped Hart up in the "Hit Man"'s signature submission move, the Sharpshooter. But before Hart could attempt to break the hold, Mr. McMahon had the official ring the bell, as if Hart had given up. Michaels was announced the winner and the new WWE Champion.

Hart broken

Realizing that he'd been tricked by the officials, Hart exploded with rage, and rumors persisted that the incident later led to a physical altercation with Mr. McMahon backstage. Hart would not return to WWE until 2006, when he was inducted into the WWE Hall of Fame.

The "Hit Man" seizes a TV monitor, venting his frustration by wreaking maximum havoc in the arena.

> **"BRET SCREWED BRET."**
>
> MR. MCMAHON

WWE Champion no longer, Bret Hart storms out of the ring area, seething with fury.

THE PIPE BOMB

Famous for entertaining interviews, CM Punk enthralled fans with a farewell tirade that lambasted the McMahon family, Superstar rivals, and the entire WWE Universe for not appreciating him enough!

"VINCE MCMAHON ... HE SURROUNDS HIMSELF WITH GLAD-HANDING, NONSENSICAL YES MEN!"

Punk cuts loose: no filter

CM Punk had nothing to lose. While he was the number-one contender for John Cena's Championship, and would be fighting Cena at *Money in the Bank 2011*, his contract was set to expire after the event, and Punk had serious reservations about re-signing with WWE. He shared those reservations with the world, delivering a scathing Pipe Bomb promo at the end of the June 27 episode of *RAW*. He claimed that, despite being "the best," his career had suffered because he was not one of Chairman Vince McMahon's favorites, like The Rock and John Cena. He also poured scorn on the WWE Universe and on the McMahon clan, describing Stephanie as "idiotic" and calling Triple H a "doofus." As he was about to tell a "personal story" about Mr. McMahon, his mic was cut off.

"OH, HEY, LET ME GET SOMETHING STRAIGHT. THOSE OF YOU WHO ARE CHEERING ME RIGHT NOW, YOU ARE JUST AS BIG A PART OF ME LEAVING AS ANYTHING ELSE!"

"I DON'T HATE YOU, JOHN. I DON'T EVEN DISLIKE YOU ... I LIKE YOU A HELL OF A LOT MORE THAN I LIKE MOST PEOPLE IN THE BACK. I HATE THIS IDEA THAT YOU'RE THE BEST. BECAUSE YOU'RE NOT. I'M THE BEST. I'M THE BEST IN THE WORLD!"

No laughing matter—John Cena is decidedly unamused by what CM Punk has to say.

As he promised, Punk won the WWE Championship, then bolted through the audience. He stopped just long enough to blow Mr. McMahon a kiss.

Bizarre Moves

GREEN MIST

With the official distracted, Tajiri blinds his opponent by spraying a noxious green mist into his face.

Mankind accessorizes Mr. Socko, so both himself and his glove puppet look the part as guest referees.

MANDIBLE CLAW

When Mankind's hand is encased in a smelly sock, his signature Mandible Claw move becomes even more disgusting for the man on the recieving end, Big Show.

48

PIT STOP

The Nasty Boys live up to their name when they subject opponents to their Pit Stop. Saggs drives a helpless foe's face into Knobbs' whiffy armpit.

Smacking his arm into position, Santino Marella delights the fans by adding a colorful snake sleeve for his signature Cobra punch.

COBRA

The deadly Cobra has put many of Marella's in-ring opponents on the canvas.

BRUNO's record TITLE runs

Bruno Sammartino has the longest WWE Championship reign in WWE history, holding the title for almost eight years, from May 17, 1963, to January 18, 1971. Equally impressive was the fact that he captured the title a second time just two years later and held it for another three and half years, from December 10, 1973, to April 10, 1977. Sammartino was WWE Champion for more than a decade, a record no one has come close to since.

"BRUNO WAS MIKE TYSON, MUHAMMAD ALI, HULK HOGAN, BROCK LESNAR, ALL ROLLED UP INTO ONE."

PAUL HEYMAN

EXTREMELY SHORT TITLE MATCH

Sammartino defeats WWE Champion Buddy Rodgers in an astounding 48 seconds to win the title.

EXTREMELY PAINFUL TITLE DEFENSE

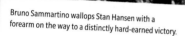

Bruno Sammartino wallops Stan Hansen with a forearm on the way to a distinctly hard-earned victory.

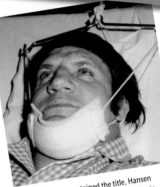

While Sammartino retained the title, Hansen fractured the champion's neck, putting him in the hospital for over a month.

Sammartino's two title reigns were so long that fans thought he'd never lose. The crowd was stunned when Superstar Billy Graham pinned him to end his second, and final, reign as WWE Champion.

EXTREMELY SHOCKING DEFEAT

EXTREMELY SCARY OPPONENTS

George "The Animal" Steele was known for his hairy back, green tongue, and for snacking on turnbuckles. A wild man in the ring, he pushed Sammartino to the limit in several title matches.

Gorilla Monsoon was the first challenger for Sammartino's WWE Championship. He battled the champ to numerous 60-minute, time-limited draws, but never got over the hump to capture the title.

RUNNING THE GAUNTLET

A Gauntlet Match doesn't happen often in WWE. Two Superstars or teams compete in a bout, and the winner immediately has to face a new opponent. The process continues through a set number of contenders. It's a massive challenge to run the gauntlet and make it to the end.

With the help of Shawn Michaels, Triple H was able to make fall guys out of Mr. McMahon cheerleaders the Spirit Squad.

Tag team turmoil

Armageddon 2003 featured a Tag Team Turmoil Match, effectively a six-team Gauntlet Match, for the World Tag Team Championship. Current holders The Dudley Boyz did not have to run the complete gauntlet (they entered fifth), so they thought they had won after eliminating the last two teams. But *RAW* General Manager Eric Bischoff had an unpleasant surprise for the champions—he introduced a seventh team to the match: Evolution stablemates Ric Flair and Batista. The fresh duo made short work of the champs, with Batista pinning D-Von Dudley after a vicious Batista Bomb.

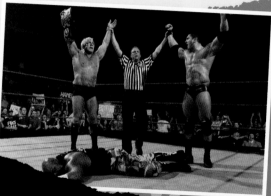

A gauntlet leads to a reunion

Through early 2006, Mr. McMahon was dealing with two insubordinate Superstars—Triple H and Shawn Michaels—and he was using the five-man Spirit Squad to hand out punishment. He forced Triple H to face the Spirit Squad's five members in a 5-on-1 Gauntlet Match. But Mr. McMahon was not satisfied with a traditional Gauntlet Match. He dismissed the official and sent Spirit Squad members one at a time to attack Triple H. "The Game" held his own when it was one-on-one and even two-on-one, but four-on-one proved too much. At Mr. McMahon's direction, the villainous cheerleaders were set to wrap a chair around Triple H's neck, but Michaels emerged and helped Triple H fend off the Squad, reuniting D-Generation X, to the delight of the WWE Universe and the chagrin of Mr. McMahon.

Seth Rollins hoists John Cena onto his shoulders to use Cena's own Attitude Adjustment finisher move against him.

Pushing Kingston to the limit

The WWE Universe wanted to see Kofi Kingston compete for the WWE Championship at *WrestleMania*, but Mr. McMahon did not want to give Kingston the opportunity he clearly deserved. To earn the shot, Mr. McMahon forced Kingston to compete in a Gauntlet Match on *SmackDown*. With the WWE Universe cheering him on, Kingston defeated Sheamus, Cesaro, Rowan, Samoa Joe, and Randy Orton to win the title opportunity—or so he thought. Instead, Mr. McMahon changed the rules at the last minute and made an exhausted Kingston fight a sixth match, against WWE Champion Daniel Bryan. The exhausted Kingston was no match for Bryan, so his title shot was denied for another week.

The 60-minute man

RAW, February 19, 2018, opened with a Gauntlet Match to decide the number-one contender for the Universal Championship. Seth Rollins and Roman Reigns started off the gauntlet. After 30 minutes, Rollins managed to outlast Reigns' power and eke out a rollup pinfall. Rollins then had to face John Cena. For an additional 30 minutes, Rollins was dominated by Cena's strength. He kicked out of multiple pinfall attempts, and to fans' amazement managed to defeat Cena and advance to a third match. Rollins had now competed for more than 60 minutes. Rollins couldn't win his third match, against Elias, but the WWE Universe was mightily impressed by his bravery and stamina.

Kofi Kingston hits Sheamus with a high crossbody move on his way to winning five matches in a grueling Gauntlet Match.

Alicia Fox nails Bayley with a kick in a Gauntlet Match to determine the number-one contender for the *RAW* Women's Championship.

> "WHEN HE SUMMONS THE DEMON KING, IT'S LIKE A WHOLE DIFFERENT PERSON."
> COREY GRAVES

Finn Bálor had won championships around the world when he joined the NXT roster. He became the longest-reigning NXT Champion in history and captured the Universal Championship. He also captured the fans' imagination with his scary Demon persona.

Finn BáLOr

King for a day

Finn Bálor had never competed on *RAW* or *SmackDown*—WWE plucked him straight from NXT. Bálor proved they'd made the right choice by winning two matches on his *RAW* debut to earn a shot at the new Universal Championship. At *SummerSlam 2016*, Bálor shocked Seth Rollins to become the first Universal Champion. Even more impressive, Bálor suffered a debilitating injury thanks to a Rollins powerbomb onto a ring barrier. Bálor fought through the pain to win. Unfortunately, he had to give up the title the next day, making him just a one-day champion.

The Demon flies through the air to drop Seth Rollins on his way to becoming WWE's first-ever Universal Champion.

The Coup de Grace

All Superstars have their signature finishers, but Bálor's Coup de Grace is one of the most devastating. He incapacitates his opponent with a variety of aerial maneuvers and grappling moves, until he is prone on the mat. Bálor then climbs to the top turnbuckle and jumps off, with both of his boots driving his full weight onto his downed foe's chest. From then on, the three count is generally just a formality.

54

The Demon emerges

Facing Finn Bálor in a match is already a daunting task, but Bálor can significantly increase the fear when he brings out the Demon. Covering his body with intricate designs, a terrifying persona emerges, and Bálor reaches a different level of aggression. At *SummerSlam 2017*, Bray Wyatt thought he had the sinister edge, but he was overwhelmed by the Demon, losing the match to a devastating Coup de Grace.

One beats two

Almost three years after having to forfeit the Universal Championship due to injury, Finn Bálor was looking to return to championship form. It seemed unlikely to happen at *Elimination Chamber 2019*, as Bálor had to challenge both Intercontinental Champion Bobby Lashley and his hype man, Lio Rush, in a Two-on-One Handicap Match. But Bálor has consistently overcome long odds throughout his career, and that night would be no different, as he pinned Rush to capture the Intercontinental Title for the first time.

Brock Lesnar
286 lb (130 kg)

Big Show
383 lb (174 kg)

The old saying, "The ring isn't big enough for these two," proved prescient during a WWE Championship Match between Brock Lesnar and Big Show.

ring Busters

Clash of the titans
WWE Champion Brock Lesnar faced a giant challenge defending his title against Big Show, the "World's Largest Athlete." The two massive competitors punished each other with punches and kicks, and Big Show thought he had the match won when he planted Lesnar with a devastating chokeslam.

Top rope turmoil

After Lesnar kicked out of a pinfall attempt at two, Show decided to take things to the next level, climbing to the second turnbuckle to get even more elevation on a second chokeslam and put the champion away. Lesnar was able to reverse the move and turn it into a Superplex off the top turnbuckle.

"I WONDER WHAT THAT REGISTERED ON THE RICHTER SCALE?"

MICHAEL COLE

Total destruction

As Lesnar and Show came crashing to the mat, the ring was unable to withstand the impact of their combined weight of 800 lb (363 kg). Exploding in all directions, the ropes collapsed, the ring posts tumbled, and the official was knocked off his feet. After a moment of stunned silence, the WWE Universe roared its approval.

Competitors are eliminated from a Royal Rumble Match when they are tossed over the top rope and both feet touch the floor. For almost a decade, Kofi Kingston has engineered some of the most over-the-top saves ever seen to prevent elimination and stay in the contest.

2012

Thrown out head first, Kingston walks on his hands until he can drop his feet back onto the ring steps and return to the Royal Rumble Match.

KOFi KiNgSTON'S SPECTaCULaR SaVeS

2013

2014

Dumped onto a barricade by Rusev, but not yet eliminated, Kingston makes a spectacular leap from the barricade to the ring.

After landing on the announcers' desk, Kingston uses an announcer's chair like a pogo stick to hop across the floor and back to the ring.

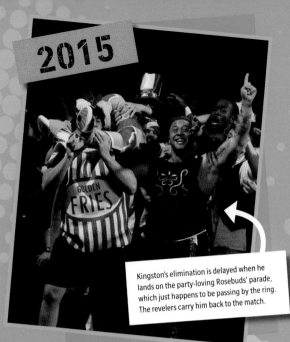

2015

Kingston's elimination is delayed when he lands on the party-loving Rosebuds' parade, which just happens to be passing by the ring. The revelers carry him back to the match.

2016

Kingston's New Day teammate Big E is on hand to give Kingston a piggyback ride to ensure he avoids elimination.

"HE IS THE MOST INNOVATIVE MAN IN *ROYAL RUMBLE* HISTORY!"

MICHAEL COLE

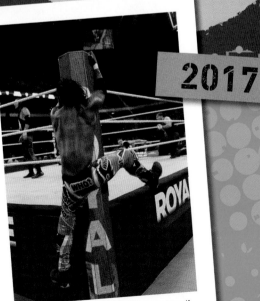

2017

Kingston hangs onto the ring post in order to stop himself from falling and get back in the match.

2018

A handy plate of pancakes prevents Kingston's right foot from touching the floor—keeping him in the Rumble.

Paging Dr. austin

Mr. McMahon was already in the hospital recuperating from an attack by Kane and Undertaker. However, the WWE Chairman's troubles were only just beginning ...

"I'LL TAKE IT FROM HERE, NURSE ..."
"DOCTOR" STONE COLD STEVE AUSTIN

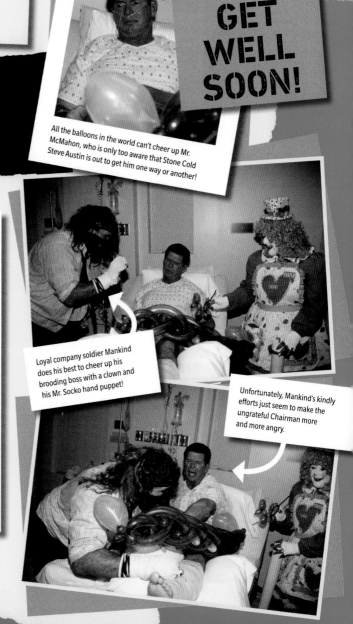

GET WELL SOON!

All the balloons in the world can't cheer up Mr. McMahon, who is only too aware that Stone Cold Steve Austin is out to get him one way or another!

Loyal company soldier Mankind does his best to cheer up his brooding boss with a clown and his Mr. Socko hand puppet!

Unfortunately, Mankind's kindly efforts just seem to make the ungrateful Chairman more and more angry.

Doctor's orders

Mr. McMahon was in bad shape. He thought Kane and Undertaker were his allies in his ongoing war with Stone Cold Steve Austin, but Mr. McMahon had angered "The Brothers of Destruction" and they assaulted him, injuring his leg and putting him in the hospital. While he recovered from his injuries, Mr. McMahon was afraid that Austin would find him and seek revenge. Mankind tried to take the Chairman's mind off his worries in his own special way, but to no avail. McMahon's fears proved well-founded—a doctor turned out to be Austin in disguise. " The Texas Rattlesnake" leaped on the bedridden Chairman, leaving him in a crumpled heap on the floor!

"THIS IS GONNA HURT YOU A LOT MORE THAN IT'S GONNA HURT ME!"

STONE COLD STEVE AUSTIN

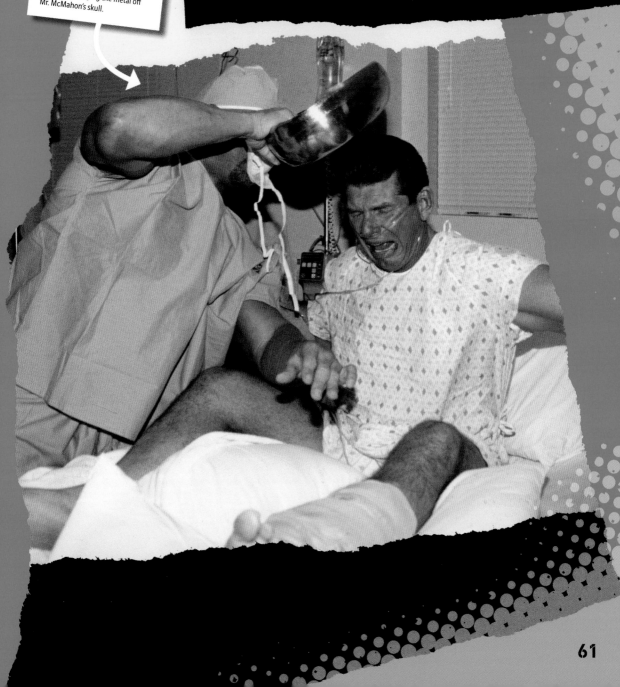

Dr. Stone Cold finds a new use for a bedpan, clanging the metal off Mr. McMahon's skull.

raw takeOver

Daniel Bryan and the WWE Universe were sick and tired of the ways The Authority's Triple H and Stephanie McMahon—WWE's power couple—were abusing their position. Bryan and his legions of fans decided to take matters into their own hands ...

Speechless with anger, Triple H and Stephanie look on helplessly as they lose control of *RAW*.

The YES! movement takes hold

The Authority wanted to keep Daniel Bryan down because it did not see him as a suitably stylish standard-bearer for WWE. Triple H wouldn't even agree to face Bryan at *WrestleMania 30*. So Bryan decided to occupy *RAW* until he got what he wanted. He didn't do it alone: the ring and area around it were filled with loyal fans of Bryan's YES! Movement, preventing the show from continuing. Enraged, Triple H was forced to promise Bryan that if he beat Triple H at *WrestleMania*, Bryan's name would be entered in the main event—the WWE World Heavyweight Championship Match—that night. The Championship Match would thus be a Triple Threat Match, featuring Randy Orton, Batista, and Daniel Bryan.

Power to the people—Triple H wants the occupiers arrested, but security cannot handle the sheer numbers filling the ring and surrounding area.

"YOU GET YOUR DEAL. GET OUT OF MY RING AND I'M GONNA END THIS AT *WRESTLEMANIA!*"

TRIPLE H

THe DeaDMaN's rUN

Undertaker achieved one of the most impressive feats in sports entertainment history by winning 21 *WrestleMania* matches in a row. Each time "The Deadman" took on WWE's greatest competitors in these highly charged events, he vanquished them the way only Undertaker could: laying each one low Tombstone after Tombstone, terrifying Superstars and the WWE Universe.

WM7

The impressive streak began at *WrestleMania VII* with a dominant victory over future Hall of Famer "Superfly" Jimmy Snuka.

WM13

"The Deadman" won the WWE Championship at *WrestleMania* for the one and only time, defeating Sycho Sid at *WrestleMania 13*.

WM14

Facing, and defeating, his younger brother Kane at *WrestleMania XIV* was perhaps Undertaker's toughest *WrestleMania* challenge.

WM15

Undertaker took the soul of the Big Boss Man at *WrestleMania XV*— the first time Hell in a Cell featured at *WrestleMania*.

WM17

Undertaker made it 10 wins in a row by defeating Ric Flair at *WrestleMania X-Seven*.

WM23

A big boot to the face of Batista helped Undertaker stop "The Animal" and win the World Heavyweight Championship at *WrestleMania 23*.

WM24

WrestleMania XXIV closed with "The Deadman" defeating Edge for the World Heavyweight Title.

WM26

In one of the greatest matches in *WrestleMania* history, Undertaker defeated Shawn Michaels and ended the career of "The Heartbreak Kid."

WM28

The third *WrestleMania* bout between Triple H and Undertaker was a brutal Hell in a Cell Match that took the streak to 20-nil!

WM30

The WWE Universe was stunned when Brock Lesnar finally ended the run at *WrestleMania 30*.

KANE

"TONIGHT I WILL BURN THE FLESH FROM YOUR BODY."

KANE

He first came to WWE more than 20 years ago, seeking revenge on his brother, Undertaker. But Kane has stuck around, bringing chaos and inflicting pain on every Superstar he can. When Kane does form an alliance, it doesn't last—before long, the "Big Red Monster" reveals his demonic side and stabs his partners in the back.

Ordeal by fire

WWE Hall of Fame announcer Jim Ross was understandably trepidatious before his interview with Kane, but JR wanted to find out why the "Big Red Monster" was so angry and violent. Kane warned his interviewer that if he thought JR was mocking him at all, he would set the announcer on fire. JR was only trying to help convey Kane's weird story to the WWE Universe, but Kane didn't see it that way. He poured gasoline on JR and set him on fire.

A split personality

From 2013 through 2015, the WWE Universe saw a new side of Kane. He donned a suit and tie to become Director of Operations for Triple H's Authority faction. Triple H's protégé and WWE Champion Seth Rollins didn't trust Kane, and with good reason: Demon Kane suddenly reemerged and attacked him! Corporate Kane bizarrely claimed to have no knowledge of Demon Kane's actions. For weeks, Rollins saw double—a well-dressed Kane that backed him, and a "Big Red Monster" that attacked him. Eventually, Rollins pinned Demon Kane, causing Corporate Kane to lose his position with The Authority.

A demonic chokeslam

RAW General Manager Eric Bischoff assumed he would get respect from the roster. Not so from Kane. Angry that Bischoff had added a stipulation to Kane's championship match with Triple H that forced the "Big Red Monster" to unmask, Kane grabbed the GM by the throat and chokeslammed him off the stage onto the floor of the arena.

Leap of Faith

20 FT

"SHANE MCMAHON PROPELLED HIMSELF OFF THE TOP OF THAT SCAFFOLDING USING HIS OWN BODY LIKE A HUMAN MISSILE AND THERE YOU SEE THE REMAINS OF THE 500-POUND BIG SHOW!"

JIM ROSS

Big Show thinks that Shane McMahon is running away from him by climbing up some scaffolding ...

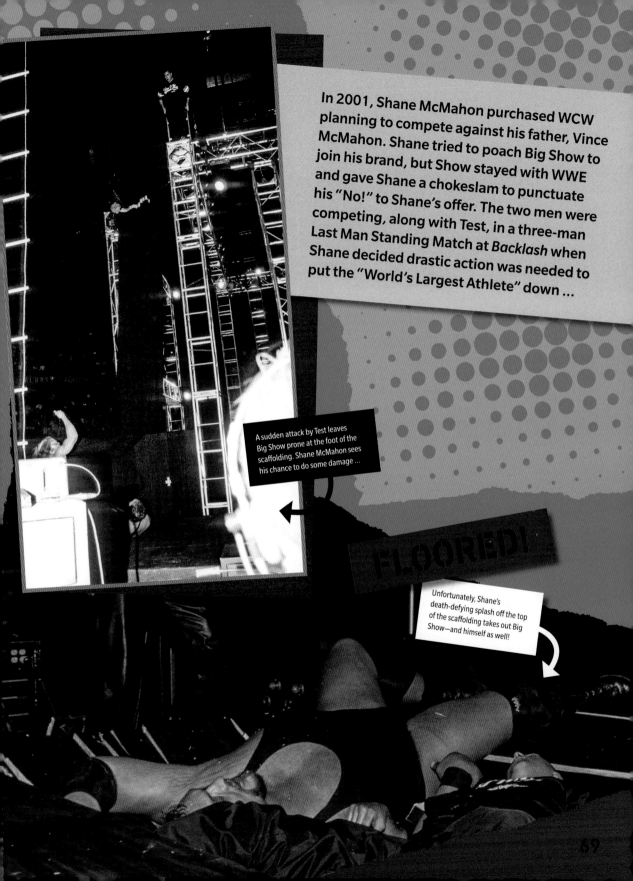

In 2001, Shane McMahon purchased WCW planning to compete against his father, Vince McMahon. Shane tried to poach Big Show to join his brand, but Show stayed with WWE and gave Shane a chokeslam to punctuate his "No!" to Shane's offer. The two men were competing, along with Test, in a three-man Last Man Standing Match at *Backlash* when Shane decided drastic action was needed to put the "World's Largest Athlete" down ...

A sudden attack by Test leaves Big Show prone at the foot of the scaffolding. Shane McMahon sees his chance to do some damage ...

FLOORED!

Unfortunately, Shane's death-defying splash off the top of the scaffolding takes out Big Show—and himself as well!

eXtreme RULeS

For more than a decade, WWE has held an annual event named *Extreme Rules.* The event has become synonymous with hard-hitting, extreme action, but it's also had its share of bizarre moments as well.

> ## "NUNCHUKS AGAINST A BARBED-WIRE 2X4?... YEAH, AMBROSE IS A LITTLE OUTGUNNED HERE!"
> JOHN LAYFIELD

Down and dirty—Vickie and Chavo Guerrero Jr. are covered in filth during their Handicap Hog Pen Match against "Santina" Morello.

In the doo-doo

The inaugural *Extreme Rules* event in 2009 featured some tough matches, but the strangest was the Handicap Hog Pen Match. It took place in a mud-filled pig pen. General Manager of *RAW* Vickie Guerrero (along with her unwilling nephew, Superstar Chavo Guerrero Jr.) showed up wearing her crown and an elegant gown to defend her Miss WrestleMania title against "Santina" Marella, supposedly Santino Marella's twin sister. All three combatants soon found themselves covered in muck. Chavo was taken out when "Santina" dumped a bucket of slop over him and then punched his bucket-covered head. "She" then pinned Vickie to become the new Miss WrestleMania! Vickie was so furious that she attacked Chavo and they both ended up rolling in the mire.

Tale of the tape

John Cena and Batista's intense rivalry in 2010 led to a Last Man Standing Match at *Extreme Rules*. In this match, pinning wasn't enough—you had to beat your opponent so badly that he couldn't get to his feet for a 10 count. With Cena and Batista two of WWE's toughest, it was hard to imagine either one not responding to a 10 count. So John Cena took extreme measures to win the match and retain his WWE Championship: He grabbed Batista's legs, pulled them past a ring post, and duct-taped them together. Batista couldn't get free before the official counted 10, so Cena was declared the winner.

Ties that bind—finding yet another use for duct tape, John Cena wraps up Batista's legs, making it impossible for him to beat the official's 10 count.

Taking over the asylum

Dean Ambrose was given the opportunity to face Chris Jericho at *Extreme Rules 2016* in a match of his choosing. He created the Asylum Match. What initially looked like a typical Steel Cage Match, the Asylum had various items hanging above the cage that could be retrieved and used as weapons. Ambrose beat Jericho about the chest with nunchucks and then whipped "Y2J" with a strap. Jericho tried to incapacitate Ambrose by putting him in a straightjacket, but Ambrose fought back, slammed Jericho onto a pile of thumbtacks, and pinned him after a Dirty Deeds move.

Giving some stick

Defending her *RAW* Women's Championship at *Extreme Rules 2017*, Alexa Bliss faced Bayley in a Kendo Stick On a Pole Match. A kendo stick was hung in one corner of the ring, and the first woman to retrieve it could legally use it as a weapon. Bayley grabbed it first but seemed conflicted about using it. Bliss snared the stick from Bayley and showed no hesitation. She thrashed her challenger. Bayley fought back but was too weak to pin Bliss. Bayley gave her one more whack with the stick, followed up with a DDT, and pinned Bayley to keep her title.

The New Day reigns

At *SummerSlam 2015*, The New Day captured the WWE Tag Team Championship for the second time in their career. They did not relinquish the titles for almost 16 months, setting a tag team record by holding on to the championship for 483 days.

Intense rivalry

One of the many teams that failed to successfully challenge The New Day during their record-breaking run was The Usos. Brothers Jimmy and Jey Uso challenged The New Day at the 2016 *Royal Rumble*. Two incredibly powerful moves by Big E saved the match for The New Day. First, he scooped up Jimmy Uso outside the ring and drove him into the ringside barrier. Even more impressively, he caught Jey Uso as he flew off the top turnbuckle for a top-rope splash and nailed him with a Big Ending to win the match.

A close call

The New Day entered the December 12, 2016 episode of *RAW* only needing to win a Triple Threat Match to tie Demolition's record championship reign. After The New Day squeaked out a victory, they launched a massive celebration in the locker room, inviting everyone and anyone. But they accidentally sprayed *RAW* Commissioner Stephanie McMahon with champagne. As a result, the vindictive McMahon forced them to defend their titles again that night in a second Triple Threat Match. The New Day managed a second victory in one night, ensuring the record would be set.

"DON'T YOU DARE BE SOUR!"

THE NEW DAY

The Demolition men

What made The New Day's record reign so impressive is how long the previous mark had stood. Demolition had previously held the longest tag team reign, and their record had lasted for more than 27 years. Ax and Smash were a dominant tag team in their day—they intimidated opponents with their leather-studded ring gear and overwhelmed teams with their brutal power moves, including their signature move, the Demolition Decapitation.

FaMiLY FeuDs

Mr. McMahon gets down with the kids, bashing son Shane with a garbage can at *WrestleMania X-Seven*.

Families don't always get along—and when that happens in WWE, it can lead to some extremely intense in-ring confrontations ...

The McMahons

WWE Chairman Mr. McMahon has had a stormy relationship with all of his family. He's argued with his wife and fought both of his children in pay-per-view bouts. Shane and Stephanie have battled him for control of the company—as well as competing for his approval.

Stephanie and Shane McMahon's rivalry was so intense, they just couldn't co-exist on the same show. So Stephanie ran *RAW*, while Shane was put in charge of *SmackDown*.

The rivalry between Bret and Owen Hart got so intense, they needed a Steel Cage Match to settle it.

The Harts

When Bret "Hit Man" Hart became a WWE Championship contender in the early 1990s, most of his family were proud. The one exception was his brother Owen Hart. Owen became a top contender for Bret's title, beating him at *WrestleMania X* hours before Bret pinned Yokozuna to become WWE Champion. The two battled for years, until they finally put their animosity aside to form the new Hart Foundation with brothers-in-law Davy Boy Smith, Jim "The Anvil" Neidhart, and Brian Pillman.

"I AM GOING TO BE THE BELLA THAT EVERYONE IS TALKING ABOUT. AND YOU? YOU'RE JUST GOING TO BE SOME MEMORY ..."

NIKKI BELLA TO HER SISTER BRIE

The Bellas

For most of their careers, the Bella Twins have assisted each other whenever needed. However, in 2014, the two fell out, culminating in a match at *Hell in a Cell*, where the losing sister would be forced to be the personal assistant of the winner for 30 days. Nikki won and eventually captured the WWE Divas Championship with the help of Brie, healing their rift.

Brie Bella drops her sister Nikki with a facebuster.

With Edge out of action and the World Title in his grasp, Jeff is stunned by Matt's intervention.

The Hardys

Matt and Jeff Hardy are a sibling tag team that fell out spectacularly. It all started at the 2009 *Royal Rumble*, when Matt cost Jeff the World Title by smacking him with a steel chair. At *WrestleMania XXV*, they pulverized each other in an Extreme Rules Match. In *SmackDown*'s first-ever Stretcher Match, Matt whacked Jeff with a steel chair to get him onto the wheeled stretcher, up a ramp, and across the finish line for the win. Jeff got revenge at *Backlash* in an I Quit Match. He strapped Matt to a table and then prepared to Swanton Bomb him from off a ladder. Helpless, Matt said he was sorry and uttered the all-important words: "I quit!"

MaN ON FiRe!

Mick Foley entered *WrestleMania 22* hoping to make a real *WrestleMania* impact. And Edge helped him do just that!

Fire hazard!

Mick Foley wanted to punctuate his Hall of Fame career with a signature moment at *WrestleMania*, so he challenged "The Rated-R Superstar" Edge to a Hardcore Match. The two men (as well as Lita, who accompanied Edge to the ring) used chairs wrapped in barbed wire, a baseball bat, and tables, but Edge and Lita took things a little bit too far. Edge set up a table outside the ring and Lita set it on fire. Foley was balanced precariously on the ring apron when Edge speared him straight through the flaming table.

"MY GOD, MICK FOLEY'S FLESH MAY BE SEARED, SPEARED THROUGH THE TABLE!"
JOEY STYLES

LiTa

Throughout her WWE career, Lita excited passionate reactions from fans. As a member of Team Xtreme, they boisterously cheered her daredevil style and aerial maneuvers. When she aligned with "Rated R Superstar" Edge, she became one of the most hated Superstars in WWE. Through it all, she showed no fear, willing to mix it up with any man in the ring.

Flying high

Back in 2000, it was rare to see women compete in the main event of *RAW*, so Lita was a trailblazer when she faced Stephanie McMahon for the Women's Championship on August 21, 2000. Lita used her superior training to toss McMahon around the ring, even though McMahon had both husband Triple H and Kurt Angle in her corner to even up matters. In the end, Lita nailed McMahon with a top-rope moonsault, becoming Women's Champion for the first time.

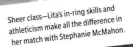

Sheer class—Lita's in-ring skills and athleticism make all the difference in her match with Stephanie McMahon.

Cruel games

In 2004, the WWE Universe was shocked by a series of events surrounding Lita. First, caught in a love triangle with Matt Hardy and Kane, Lita allegedly became pregnant with Kane's satanic spawn. Then, she lost the baby due to a physical altercation with the monstrous Snitsky. Showing no limits to his cruelty, Snitsky crashed an interview Lita was having carrying a baby and mocked her. He then punted the baby into the arena, where the crowd tried desperately to catch it. Thankfully, it turned out to be a doll.

Courting controversy

Lita and her partner Edge were two competitors who were unafraid to push things to the limit. When Edge kicked off 2006 by winning the WWE Championship, he and Lita thought the best way to celebrate was to share an intimate moment live on *RAW*. Edge and Lita shocked everyone in the arena by disrobing and getting into a bed in the middle of the ring. Thankfully, Ric Flair entered the ring and interrupted proceedings.

a Quitter Never wins!

This grueling match isn't about pinfalls—it's about pain. It's the ultimate humiliation—forcing an opponent to scream "I quit" for all the world to hear. I Quit Matches have ended careers and settled some of WWE's most intense rivalries.

Guest referee "Rowdy" Roddy Piper shoves a mic into Bob Backlund's face to see if he wants to quit during his match with Bret Hart at *WrestleMania XI*.

"EVEN THOUGH YOU HAVE ONE EAR, THE ROCK HAS TWO, WHICH MEANS ... THE ROCK IS GOING TO HEAR YOU SCREAM 'I QUIT!'"

THE ROCK CRUELLY TAUNTS MANKIND

The Rock is rumbled
The Rock and Mankind clashed at *Royal Rumble 1999* in an I Quit Match for the WWE Championship. The Rock took match action further than ever seen before, blasting Mankind with chair shots, many while Mankind's hands were handcuffed behind his back. Mankind finally collapsed to the ground and seemed to scream "I quit!" But shockingly, The Rock's associates had played a recording of Mankind saying the humiliating phrase to fool the ref.

Batista calls it quits

At *Over the Limit 2010*, Batista and John Cena faced each other in an I Quit Match for the WWE Championship. Cena was ready to do whatever it took to put "The Animal" down, dropping Batista with his Attitude Adjustment move onto a car. When Batista refused to quit, Cena went for the move again, planning to drop Batista off the stage. "The Animal" shouted "I quit" to prevent that from happening, but Cena did the move anyway. Enraged at this treatment by Cena, a heavily bandaged Batista appeared on *RAW* the next night and quit WWE altogether!

Too much for Melina

Women competed in an I Quit Match in WWE for the first time ever at *One Night Stand 2008*. Former allies Beth Phoenix and Melina had built up such enmity between them that an I Quit Match seemed the only way to decide who was the superior Superstar. Breaking Melina's arm-bar submission move, Phoenix used her immense power to twist Melina into such a contorted, painful position that she just had to scream "I quit!"

At *Backlash 2009*, Matt Hardy shouts "I quit" rather than face brother Jeff's devastating move off a ladder. Jeff went through with a leg drop anyway!

SHOCKING RETURNS

Nothing excites the WWE Universe more than when an absent Superstar makes an overdue return to WWE.

SHAWN MICHAELS

After a back injury forced an early in-ring retirement, Shawn Michaels made a competitive return after four years away from action.

RIC FLAIR

Ric Flair returned to WWE as part owner of the organization when he secretly purchased Shane and Stephanie's company stock!

SHANE McMAHON

The WWE Universe had not seen Shane McMahon for years when he made a shock appearance in 2016 to stop his sister Stephanie from receiving the Vincent J. McMahon Legacy of Excellence award from their father, Mr. McMahon. He also wanted to challenge the WWE Chairman for control of *RAW*.

THE ROCK

BROCK LESNAR

To massive fan acclaim, in 2011, "The Most Electrifying Man in All of Entertainment" came home to WWE from Hollywood when he was chosen to host *WrestleMania XXVII*.

"FINALLY THE ROCK HAS COME BACK ... HOME!"

THE ROCK

"The Beast" had departed WWE for eight years to conquer Ultimate Fighting Championship rings. His return to WWE would bring him multiple championships and also bring an end to Undertaker's historic *WrestleMania* streak.

BRET "HIT MAN" HART

"THANK YOU SO MUCH FOR NEVER LETTING ME BE FORGOTTEN!"

BRET HART

After the Montreal Screwjob, the WWE Universe thought they'd never see Bret "Hit Man" Hart in a WWE ring again. But he returned in 2010, buried the hatchet with rival Shawn Michaels, and got revenge on Vince McMahon in a *WrestleMania* bout.

CHARLOTTE'S PERFECT NINE

In less than five years, Charlotte Flair has already set a WWE record with nine reigns as Women's Champion (one as Divas Champion, four as *RAW* Women's Champion, and four as *SmackDown* Women's Champion). Charlotte shows no signs of slowing down as she gets closer to surpassing her father Ric Flair's 16 world title reigns ...

Charlotte locks Nikki Bella in her signature Figure 8 Leglock, forcing the champion to tap out and relinquish the Divas Championship.

4-WAY CHAMP

Charlotte is the only competitor in WWE history to hold the Divas Championship and the *RAW*, *SmackDown*, and *NXT* Women's Championships.

Charlotte's first and last

Charlotte first captured gold at *Night of Champions 2015*, ending Nikki Bella's record-breaking 301-day reign as Divas Champion. Charlotte held the title through *WrestleMania 32*, expecting to defend it in a Triple Threat Match against Sasha Banks and Becky Lynch. But WWE Hall of Famer Lita made a surprise announcement that the title was being retired and replaced by the WWE Women's Championship. When Charlotte won, she entered the record books as both the last Divas Champion and the first WWE Women's Champion.

New show, more gold

The 2017 Superstar Shakeup moved Charlotte from *RAW* to *SmackDown* in April; and seven months later, Charlotte beat Natalya for the *SmackDown* Women's Title. Her 146-day reign is currently the longest in the championship's short history.

Flair proudly displays the *SmackDown* Women's Title after beating Natalya.

Queen of pay-per-view

Throughout 2016, Charlotte found herself in an ongoing rivalry with Sasha Banks for the *RAW* Women's Championship. On three 2016 episodes of *RAW*—July 25, October 3, and November 28—Banks defeated Charlotte for the title. But on each subsequent pay-per-view event, Charlotte took advantage of the bright spotlight to take back her title.

> "I NEVER **DREAMED** OF SUCCESS ... I **WORKED** FOR IT."
>
> CHARLOTTE FLAIR

Charlotte defeats Asuka to claim the *SmackDown* Women's Championship on March 26, 2019.

raw power

Braun Strowman is a monster among men, and his strength and power have become the stuff of legend. No object seems too big for Braun Strowman to toss around!

291

Thinking that Kevin Owens is hiding in a limo backstage, Braun Strowman rips the door off the vehicle to get to him.

Jinder Mahal, Sumil Singh, and Kevin Owens are not safe from Strowman's rage as he flips over the stage all three are standing on!

BROKEN RING

"The Monster Among Men" scoops up Kane for a running Powerslam ...

Underestimating his own strength, Strowman slams Kane right through the ring!

Don't fire "The Monster"
Looking to exercise a little authority, *RAW* General Manager Kurt Angle threatened to fire Braun Strowman if he didn't obey orders. The tactic backfired, as an enraged Strowman flipped over the massive truck that hauls WWE's television control studio.

STEP#aNie's Vegas weDDiNg

The stage was set for a beautiful and happy event. Mr. McMahon was proudly giving his daughter away in a wedding ceremony where she was set to marry Test. Or so he thought ...

Video nasty

As Stephanie and Test were about to tie the knot, Triple H interrupted the ceremony. He had brought the "happy couple" a gift neither of them wanted. It was video proof that he had married Stephanie in Las Vegas while she was unconscious—Triple H had faked her voice for all the crucial responses! With the wedding ruined, a seething Mr. McMahon looked to get revenge on his "son-in-law" at *Armageddon 1999*. But all he got was betrayal—his baby girl shocked all by turning on her father and siding with Triple H, making the marriage official.

Triple H places a ring onto Stephanie's finger, making the marriage official—despite the fact that she has passed out!

The entire wedding party is shocked and horrified by Triple H's video evidence!

Stephanie embraces Triple H, completing the stunning betrayal of her father and signaling the beginning of the McMahon-Helmsley Era in WWE.

"I'M NOT DADDY'S LITTLE GIRL ANYMORE!"

STEPHANIE MCMAHON

He had traveled the world wowing audiences with innovative moves and heaps of high-flying energy. The signing of Ricochet was perhaps the most anticipated arrival in NXT history. The WWE Universe soon discovered that all the hype was real!

RICOCHET

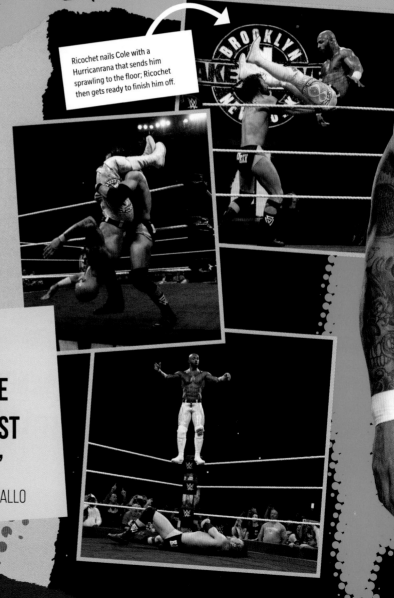

Ricochet nails Cole with a Hurricanrana that sends him sprawling to the floor; Ricochet then gets ready to finish him off.

What special looks like

Adam Cole, the NXT North American Champion, tried to get under Ricochet's skin by saying that he was good but not special. Ricochet showed Cole how special he could be in a title match at *NXT Takeover: Brooklyn 4*. In a spectacular sequence to finish off the champ, Ricochet hit Cole with a leaping Hurricanrana onto the ring floor and then a top-rope 630 senton to pin the champ and win the title.

"CIRQUE DE RICOCHET IN FULL EFFECT AND HE HAS WRECKED THE REST OF THE COMPETITION!"

MAURO RANALLO

War games

Ricochet teamed with Pete Dunne and the War Raiders to challenge the Undisputed Era at NXT *Takeover: WarGames 2018*. The eight men battled in a brutal WarGames Match inside a double cage. The crucial moment of the night came when Ricochet climbed to the top of the cage and scattered all seven competitors with a double moonsault.

Here he comes—Ricochet's thrilling moonsault is about to take out seven other opponents.

There he goes—Ricochet finds himself flying through the air toward a steel ladder.

Crash landing—the ladder buckles as Ricochet smashes down on it.

Extreme pain

The 2019 Money in the Bank Match had a painful conclusion for Ricochet. During the multiman scrum to grab the briefcase above the ring, Ricochet ran afoul of "Scottish Psychopath" Drew McIntyre, who tossed Ricochet over the top rope and onto a ladder bridged across the ring to the announcers' desk. The impact dented the ladder and Ricochet as well!

TeRRiBLe taBLe MaNNers!

Being so close to the action allows WWE announcers to make great calls, but it also puts them right in the firing line. Battles between Superstars often spill out of the ring and smash announcers' tables to a splintered mess!

Big break—in a first for WWE, Diesel turns Bret "Hit Man" Hart into a weapon of mass destruction at *Survivor Series 1995*.

Out of control—Charlotte and Sasha Banks take their Hell in a Cell battle outside, with Banks on the receiving end of a powerbomb.

Aerial power—Seth Rollins flies through the air to drop an elbow on Brock Lesnar and send him through the announcers' table.

Trouble comes in threes—The Shield execute a devastating Triple Powerbomb on Undertaker, with inevitable results.

Look out below—with the WWE Universe roaring him on, Sabu leaps from the ring to land on a helpless John Cena.

ROLLINS' CRUEL CASH-IN

No *Money in the Bank* winner had ever cashed in at *WrestleMania*, instead picking spots when the champion was most vulnerable. Then Seth Rollins came along ...

"ROLLINS WITH THE HEIST OF THE CENTURY!"

MICHAEL COLE

Snatched by Seth

It was supposed to be Roman Reigns' night. By winning the 2015 *Royal Rumble*, he was guaranteed a shot at Brock Lesnar's title at *WrestleMania 31*. Lesnar dominated the match, leading the commentators to write Reigns off, but Reigns managed to come back, stunning Lesnar by tossing him into an outside ring post. As the two exhausted warriors lay on the mat, in ran Seth Rollins with his *Money in the Bank* briefcase, turning the contest into a Triple Threat Match. After stomping Reigns and pinning him, Rollins won the match, shocking the WWE Universe by stealing the WWE Championship and Roman Reigns' chance of glory.

WWE Champion "The Beast Incarnate" Brock Lesnar looks to finish challenger Roman Reigns with his signature F-5 move.

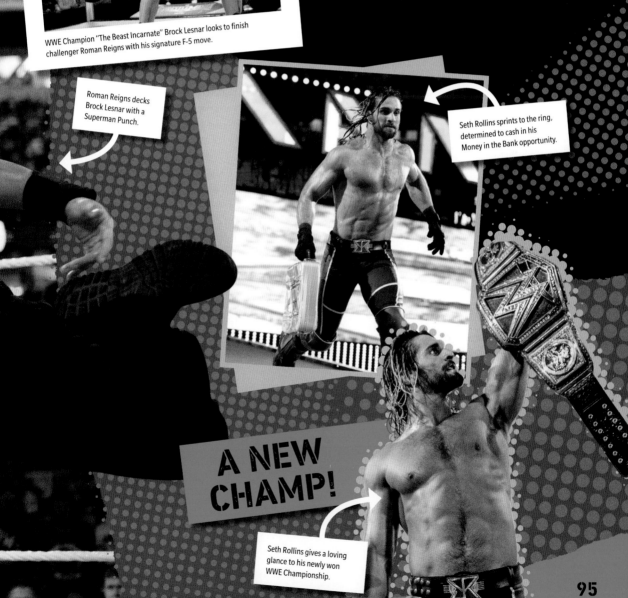

Roman Reigns decks Brock Lesnar with a Superman Punch.

Seth Rollins sprints to the ring, determined to cash in his Money in the Bank opportunity.

A NEW CHAMP!

Seth Rollins gives a loving glance to his newly won WWE Championship.

ROYAL RUMBLE Feats

It's a real endurance test—30 (sometimes 40, or even 50) competitors battling to be the last Superstar standing. The prize is often a championship opportunity at *WrestleMania*. To outlast the rest takes superhuman effort, technical skill, and a ruthless will to win.

The Big Red Monster rules

In 2001, Kane managed to get rid of 11 opponents all by himself. Entering the match at #6, "The Big Red Monster" eliminated six competitors in a row and then continued to dominate the match until there were only two entrants remaining—himself and Stone Cold Steve Austin. Even though Kane had been in the ring for almost an hour, it took a Stone Cold stunner and three chairshots before Austin could dump Kane out of the ring. Austin set a record by winning his third Royal Rumble, but it was Kane's performance that had everyone talking.

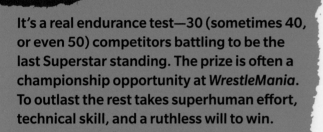

Diesel uses his superior size and strength to pummel an opponent with an elbow.

Early Dominance

The seventh entrant in the 1994 *Royal Rumble*, Diesel, was more known for being Shawn Michaels' bodyguard—but not for much longer. Four men were in the ring when "Big Daddy Cool" entered, and he tossed all of them out before the next competitor was even announced! Diesel then eliminated each of the next three competitors, running his streak to an unprecedented seven. This was just a taste of what was to come from the future multititle winner.

No WWE Superstar has eliminated as many competitors from Royal Rumble Matches as Kane.

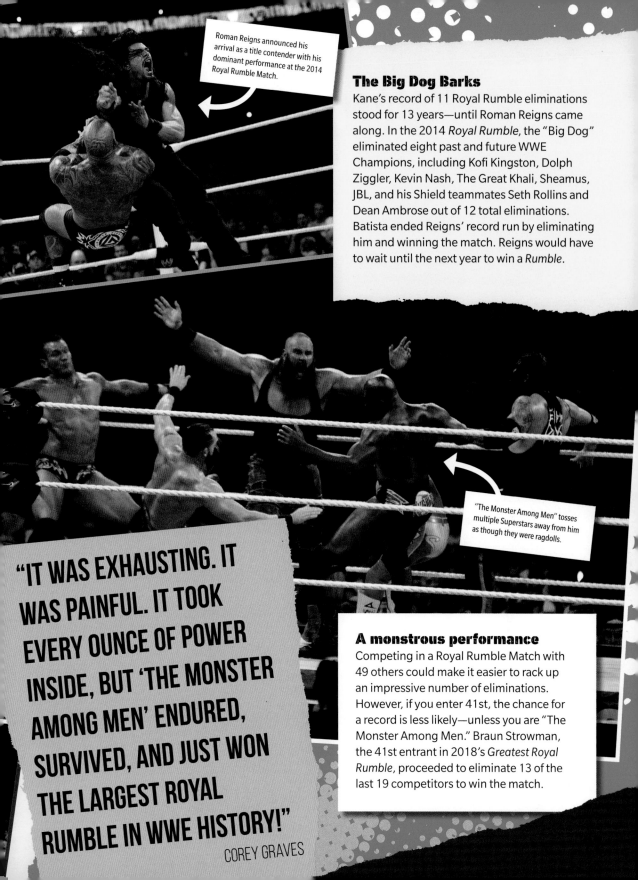

Roman Reigns announced his arrival as a title contender with his dominant performance at the 2014 Royal Rumble Match.

The Big Dog Barks

Kane's record of 11 Royal Rumble eliminations stood for 13 years—until Roman Reigns came along. In the 2014 *Royal Rumble*, the "Big Dog" eliminated eight past and future WWE Champions, including Kofi Kingston, Dolph Ziggler, Kevin Nash, The Great Khali, Sheamus, JBL, and his Shield teammates Seth Rollins and Dean Ambrose out of 12 total eliminations. Batista ended Reigns' record run by eliminating him and winning the match. Reigns would have to wait until the next year to win a *Rumble*.

"The Monster Among Men" tosses multiple Superstars away from him as though they were ragdolls.

"IT WAS EXHAUSTING. IT WAS PAINFUL. IT TOOK EVERY OUNCE OF POWER INSIDE, BUT 'THE MONSTER AMONG MEN' ENDURED, SURVIVED, AND JUST WON THE LARGEST ROYAL RUMBLE IN WWE HISTORY!"

COREY GRAVES

A monstrous performance

Competing in a Royal Rumble Match with 49 others could make it easier to rack up an impressive number of eliminations. However, if you enter 41st, the chance for a record is less likely—unless you are "The Monster Among Men." Braun Strowman, the 41st entrant in 2018's *Greatest Royal Rumble*, proceeded to eliminate 13 of the last 19 competitors to win the match.

INFERNO MATCH

Could anything in WWE be more extreme than a match in which the only way to win is to set your opponent on fire?

Brotherly hatred

The first time an Inferno Match took place in WWE, it featured the most infamous sibling rivalry in WWE history. Brothers Undertaker and Kane battled in a ring surrounded by fire, with flames shooting up with each clubbing blow. Both men attempted to drive the other into the inferno, but Undertaker finally won by driving Kane's arm into a wall of flame, setting it on fire.

Family drama is taken to a whole new level when Kane and Undertaker battle it out in a ring surrounded by scorching flames.

MVP gets burned

After a seven-year absence from WWE, the Inferno Match returned at *Armageddon 2006*. As ever, Kane was one of the competitors. His opponent, MVP, was facing the terrifying walls of fire for the first time. Kane used his experience of past Inferno Matches to push MVP's back into the fire.

That smarts!

Here are just some of the body parts that have been scorched in Inferno matches ...

ARM

FOOT

BACK

Kane gets burned at *Unforgiven 1998*.

Kane goes down in flames: *RAW*, February 22, 1999.

MVP feels the heat at *Armageddon 2006*.

Ring of fire

While there hasn't been an Inferno Match in WWE since 2007, there was a Ring of Fire Match at *SummerSlam 2013*, pitting Bray Wyatt, in his first-ever WWE match, against Kane. Surrounding the ring with flames should have kept the match a one-on-one encounter, but the members of the Wyatt Family, Luke Harper and Erick Rowan, managed to interfere anyway, helping Bray Wyatt to gain a pinfall victory.

Big TLC Trouble

In the early 2000s, rivalry for the World Tag Championships was a three-way thing: Aerial specialists The Hardy Boyz were ladder experts, The Dudley Boyz were known for putting opponents through tables, and Edge & Christian found new ways to inflict pain with chairs. TLC Matches were invented to bring all their expertise together in a single match. These bouts have become some of the most entertaining, over-the-top spectacles in all of WWE.

The Dudleys use the extra height of a ladder to make their "Wassup!" double-team move even more painful for Edge.

> "MY GOD. HAVE WE EVER SEEN ANYTHING LIKE THIS IN OUR LIVES? I KNOW I HAVEN'T. THIS IS AMAZING!"
>
> JIM ROSS

Smashing time

Six men fought in the first TLC Match at *SummerSlam 2000*, and all of them felt the pain of steel chairs, unforgiving tables, and brutal ladders. Jeff Hardy tried to nail Bubba Ray Dudley with a Swanton Bomb off a 20-foot (6.1-meter) ladder, but Dudley moved, and Jeff crashed through a pair of tables. Bubba Ray's luck ran out when Edge and Christian knocked over his ladder and he went through a stack of four tables outside the ring. Matt Hardy suffered a similar fate at the hands of D-Von Dudley. In the end, Edge & Christian were the last two standing, and they retrieved the titles to stay World Tag Team Champions.

Small is beautiful!

In one of WWE's strangest-ever matches, the diminutive Hornswoggle and El Torito met in a WeeLC Match at *Extreme Rules 2014*. It featured miniature versions of ladders, tables, and chairs, and even smaller ring announcers, officials, and commentators. Hornswoggle even put El Torito through a micro version of an announcers' table! The gigantic Jinder Mahal tried to interfere on Hornswoggle's behalf, but, with the help of Los Matadores, El Torito put Mahal through a stack of ladders and tables. He also put Hornswoggle through a small table to pin him and win the match.

Winner takes all

In late 2013, WWE decided to unify the World Heavyweight Championship and the WWE Championship into a single championship. The two titles hung above the ring in a TLC Match between Randy Orton and John Cena. Late in the contest, Orton handcuffed Cena to the bottom rope, thinking that would make it impossible for Cena to climb a ladder and retrieve the titles. Cena almost outsmarted Orton, disassembling one of the turnbuckles to take the ring ropes with him up the ladder. So Orton used the ropes to pull Cena off the ladder, sending him crashing through a table. Orton grabbed both titles to become the first WWE World Heavyweight Champion.

Hanging from the two suspended championships, John Cena finds himself incredibly vulnerable to a Randy Orton chair attack.

Asuka is ready for TLC

In her first year in WWE, Asuka showed flashes of dominance but had not reached the championship form from her NXT days. At *TLC 2019*, she had another chance to do so by facing both Becky Lynch and Charlotte Flair in a Triple Threat TLC Match for the *SmackDown* Women's Championship. She adapted well to her first TLC Match, slamming Becky off the second rope onto a ladder and powerbombing Charlotte through a table. But Becky persevered, decimating both challengers with a series of nasty chair shots. Asuka won thanks to an assist from Ronda Rousey, who knocked both Becky and Charlotte off a ladder to clear a championship path for the "Empress of Tomorrow."

THE SHIELD

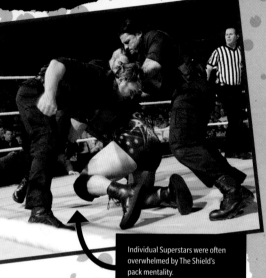

Individual Superstars were often overwhelmed by The Shield's pack mentality.

Since their debut at *Survivor Series 2012*, Dean Ambrose, Seth Rollins, and Roman Reigns, collectively known as The Shield, have imposed their will in WWE. The Shield claimed they wanted to address the injustices in WWE, but they used their strength, speed, and superior numbers to perpetrate injustices of their own.

One night, three champions

In an outrageous sequence of events, all three members of The Shield held the WWE Championship in a five-minute span on June 19, 2016. Roman Reigns was the WWE Champion heading into *Money in the Bank 2016*. His title challenger, Seth Rollins, was able to defeat Reigns in the match and regain the WWE Championship. But his celebration was short-lived. Out came Dean Ambrose, who earlier that night had won the Money in the Bank Match, guaranteeing him a title shot at the time of his choosing. After hitting Rollins with the Money in the Bank briefcase, Ambrose chose to cash in his opportunity, and he defeated Rollins, becoming the third member of The Shield to hold the title that night.

Known as the "Powerhouse of The Shield," Roman Reigns could drop even the biggest competitors out there—most impressively, Reigns overcame leukemia to return to action in 2019!

"The Lunatic Fringe" Dean Ambrose brought unpredictability to The Shield. He embraced chaos and performed maneuvers that often hurt him as much as his opponents.

"The Architect" Seth Rollins claimed to be the creator of The Shield. His focus on being the best has led to three championship reigns.

The Hounds of Justice plant John Cena with a Triple Powerbomb!

Triple trouble

Since their debut, The Shield has devastated numerous opponents with their elevated Triple Powerbomb, even when their participation in a match was outlawed. At *Survivor Series 2012*, they debuted by putting Ryback through the announcers' table with the move, helping CM Punk retain his title. Despite being banned from the match, they perpetrated the same move during Punk's *Royal Rumble 2013* title defense against The Rock. The lights in the arena had gone out, so Mr. McMahon couldn't prove it was them.

> "THERE'S NO FORCE OF NATURE ON THE EARTH THAT'S AS POWERFUL AS THE SHIELD."
>
> DEAN AMBROSE

AJ Styles stands no chance when The Shield come gunning for him!

Brotherhood over brand

In the main event of *Survivor Series 2016*, Seth Rollins and Roman Reigns fought on the *RAW* five-man team, and Dean Ambrose was one of the five Superstars representing *SmackDown*. It seemed that the former Shield teammates would battle each other that night to help settle brand supremacy. The Shield, however, had other ideas. Ambrose turned on the rest of the *SmackDown* team and helped his Shield brothers execute their patented Triple Powerbomb on AJ Styles.

extreMe weaPOns

Some WWE Superstars will do anything they can and use anything they can to win a match.

Leg-pull—Diesel grabs the artificial limb off of retired Superstar Mad Dog Vachon in order to attack Shawn Michaels.

Which would you prefer?—Mick Foley's got Mr. Socko in his right hand and a barbed-wire-covered baseball bat in his left.

Royal beatdown—"Macho King" Randy Savage uses his scepter to attack The Ultimate Warrior.

Just chill out—Nikki Bella blasts Carmella with a fire extinguisher during their No Disqualification Match at *TLC 2016*.

Right tool for the job—Triple H wields a pair of needlenose pliers as he prepares to extract Batista's nose ring in the worst way.

Bum note—Xavier Woods blasts Joey Uso with his trombone Francesca during The New Day's Hell in a Cell Match with The Usos.

Extreme Destruction

Sometimes a WWE Superstar becomes so enraged by an adversary's deeds, so incensed by perceived wrongs, that they'll take drastic, vengeful action far beyond in-ring competition. At times like these, there's no telling what havoc will ensue!

Unwelcome guest—arriving at the burial of Big Show's father, Big Boss Man claims he's only there to pay his respects.

Here comes trouble—a cement truck driven by Stone Cold Steve Austin approaches Mr. McMahon's spiffy Corvette convertible.

Flashpoint—the giant Superstar lashes out at Big Boss Man for having the nerve to interrupt such a solemn occasion.

A real showstopper—Big Boss Man causes absolute chaos, dragging both Big Show and his father's casket around the cemetery.

A full load—the boss regrets leaving the top down after "The Texas Rattlesnake" fills the car with liquid cement!

Twice the pain—after injuring The Rock so badly that he has to be loaded into an ambulance, the nWo commandeer the vehicle and drive it into a tractor trailer to further injure "The Great One."

Flaming wreck—D-Generation X's Triple H seethes with anger to see that Stone Cold Steve Austin has utterly destroyed their custom tour bus, the DX Express.

Well and truly pimped—John Cena and Cryme Tyme decide to "customize" JBL's limousine.

a Step Too Far

Superstars will use almost anything they can to gain an advantage in the ring. For some of the more inventive, weaponizing the steel ring steps is a highly effective way of beating a rival into submission.

Final finish—receiving an RKO onto the mat is a painful experience. When Orton RKOs an opponent onto ring steps, the match is over.

Face time—with Herculean strength, John Cena picks up the ring steps and tosses them at Bray Wyatt outside the ring!

Head first—Chyna steps up her game, tossing Mankind into the ring steps!

108

Flat out—in the first-ever Steel Steps Match, Erick Rowan prepares to decimate Big Show by using the steps as a middle-rope weapon.

It takes two—Brock Lesnar targets Kane's ankle by crushing it between two sets of ring steps.

Backbreaker—Batista finishes off World Heavyweight Championship contender JBL with a brutal Batista Bomb onto the ring steps.

Battling Becky

Becky "The Man" Lynch thought that leading a *SmackDown* invasion of *RAW* was a cool idea. She had to pull out all the stops to pull it off!

"The Man" strikes!

As the team representing *RAW* in the *SmackDown* Vs. *RAW* Women's Match at *Survivor Series 2018* was celebrating in the ring, cameras caught a commotion backstage. *SmackDown* Women's Champion Becky Lynch had ambushed *RAW* Women's Champion Ronda Rousey and locked her in her agonizing Dis-arm-her submission hold!

Getting backup

Becky seemed set to challenge the entire *RAW* women's team in the ring, but it was just a distraction. The *SmackDown* women's division came through the crowd to brawl in the ring.

> ## "'THE MAN' WANTED TO SEND A MESSAGE TO RONDA ROUSEY. SHE DELIVERED LOUD AND CLEAR."
>
> RENEE YOUNG

Blasting Rousey

Becky joined in the brawl but received a wicked punch from *RAW*'s Nia Jax. Having a bloody nose didn't deter Becky, who plastered Ronda with multiple chair shots before retreating through the crowd.

Normally bitter rivals, Becky and Charlotte work together to take down *RAW*'s Tamina.

BOxeD in!

A Casket Match is one of WWE's most diabolical matches. The only way to win is to entomb your opponent in the casket and slam the lid shut!

Undertaker dumps "The Ugandan Giant" Kamala into the casket before slamming down the lid and claiming the match.

RIP, Kamala!

Undertaker and Kamala competed in WWE's first-ever Casket Match—called a Coffin Match—at *Survivor Series 1992*. Kamala wanted revenge on "The Deadman" for his *SummerSlam* victory over the giant, but Kamala feared being trapped in the wooden box. He probably never got over that fear: Undertaker got him in the coffin, placed the lid over him, and nailed it in place!

Triple H drops Viscera with a Pedigree during his Handicap Casket Match against Viscera and Mideon, the only Casket Match in WWE history not to feature Undertaker or Kane.

A tale of two caskets

Yokozuna and Undertaker faced each other in two casket matches in 1994. The first was for the WWE Championship at the *Royal Rumble*. It seemed inevitable that Undertaker would seal Yokozuna in the casket, but Yokozuna's managers took advantage of the fact that Casket Matches have no disqualification and paid several Superstars to help Yokozuna win.

The two faced off in a second Casket Match at *Survivor Series*, with Undertaker out for revenge. To prevent outside interference, WWE brought a Special Outside Enforcer—TV tough guy Chuck Norris. His presence was necessary as, once again, several Superstars attempted to interfere in the match. This time they were stopped in their tracks by the *Walker: Texas Ranger* star, and Undertaker sealed Yokozuna in the casket to win.

Undertaker is overwhelmed by numerous Superstars, helping Yokozuna win his Casket Match for the WWE Championship at 1994's *Royal Rumble*.

Legendary badass Chuck Norris prevents any outside interference at *Survivor Series 1994*.

Kane and Undertaker continue to battle inside the casket—destroying it in the process!

No casket, no winner

With their storied rivalry, it's no surprise that Undertaker and Kane have met in a Casket Match. What was unique was the inconclusive result. The two brothers ended up in the casket together, battling each other. Before one of them could get out and be declared the winner, they had completely smashed up the casket. As a result, the bout was declared No Contest.

MICK FOLEY

Mick Foley's WWE journey is a tale of extreme shifts. As Mankind, he entered WWE as a deranged lunatic looking to take down Undertaker, but the fans soon embraced his goofy style. They loved all his strange characters, and they also loved Mick Foley himself, the three-time Commissioner of *RAW*.

MANKIND

DUDE LOVE

Crazy hippie Dude Love considered himself a fan favorite and sex symbol and loved to impress the ladies with his wrestling acumen.

CACTUS JACK

Deranged Cactus Jack seemed more interested in inflicting pain and suffering on his opponents than actually winning matches!

A rivalry reaches boiling point

One of the many ways Mankind brought his unique brand of violence to WWE was the invention of the Boiler Room Brawl. Two men fought in the bowels of an arena and inflicted any amount of punishment on his rival to be the first to escape the boiler room and win the match. Mankind fought in four Boiler Room Brawls, defeating Undertaker and Big Show, while losing to Triple H twice.

> ## "YOU CAN'T SATISFY EVERYBODY. IF YOU DO, YOU'RE PROBABLY DOING SOMETHING WRONG."
>
> MICK FOLEY

Which Foley?

The WWE Universe would eventually come to know the "three faces of Foley." Each face had a different approach to life and competition. After having Mankind in WWE for a few years, fans got to meet Dude Love, a free-love hippie that considered himself a sex symbol and a fan favorite. Later, both Mankind and Dude Love introduced Triple H to brawler Cactus Jack. All three of Foley's odd personas competed in the 1998 *Royal Rumble*, although they never fought each other!

Back to evil

The WWE Universe was stunned in early 2006 when Mick Foley aligned himself with the villainous couple Edge and Lita. The trio particularly targeted ECW's Tommy Dreamer and Terry Funk, along with Dreamer's wife, Beulah. All six met in an Intergender Hardcore Match at *One Night Stand* and Foley demonstrated particular brutality, punching Funk with fists wrapped in barbed wire. Foley, Edge, and Lita won the match when Edge pinned Beulah.

ASUKA'S UNDEFEATED STREAK

From her NXT debut in October 2015, no one would pin or make Asuka submit for two and a half years. That run included a record-setting 523-day reign as NXT Women's Champion. Asuka continued her winning ways on the *RAW* roster, capturing the first-ever *Women's Royal Rumble* in 2018. That earned her a shot at *SmackDown* Women's Champion Charlotte Flair at *WrestleMania 34*, where Flair finally defeated Asuka, ending her unbeaten streak at a mind-boggling 914 days.

Asuka announces her arrival at NXT with a dominant victory over Dana Brooke.

DAY 1

The colorful yet devastating Asuka stares down the competition before the match.

Day 177—Asuka captures the NXT Women's Title by defeating Bayley at *NXT Takeover: Dallas*.

DAY 177

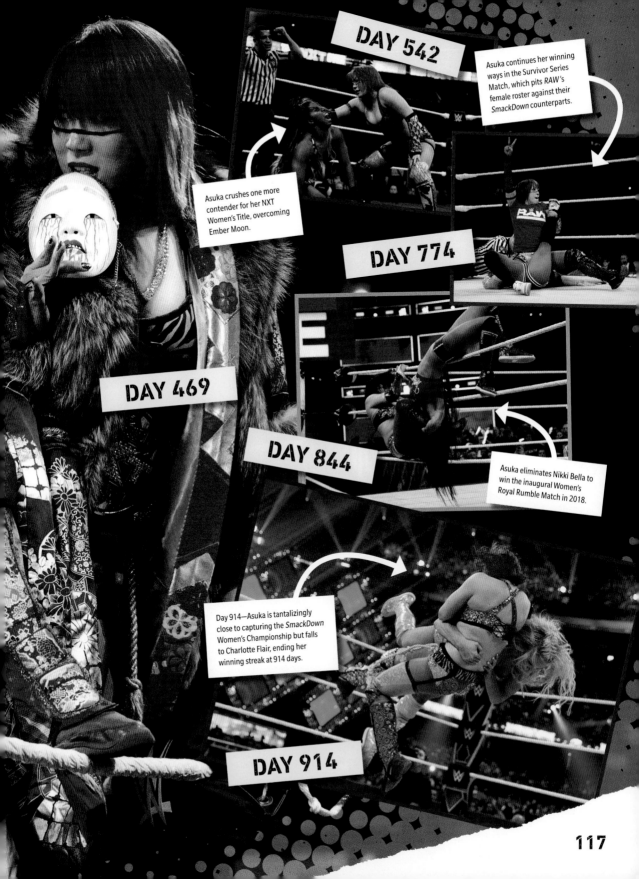

DAY 542

Asuka continues her winning ways in the Survivor Series Match, which pits *RAW's* female roster against their *SmackDown* counterparts.

Asuka crushes one more contender for her NXT Women's Title, overcoming Ember Moon.

DAY 774

DAY 469

DAY 844

Asuka eliminates Nikki Bella to win the inaugural Women's Royal Rumble Match in 2018.

Day 914—Asuka is tantalizingly close to capturing the *SmackDown* Women's Championship but falls to Charlotte Flair, ending her winning streak at 914 days.

DAY 914

FINISHED OFF!

All WWE Superstars have their signature moves to finish off opponents, but some are more extreme than others ...

Order of the boot—Shane's Brogue Kick drops WWE Champion Daniel Bryan for a record-setting title victory at WrestleMania XXVIII.

Out go the lights—Big Show's devastating WMD punch helps John Laurinaitis defeat John Cena at Over the Limit 2012.

Going down—Goldburg lays out Kevin Owens with a Jackhammer on the way to the Universal Championship in 2017.

One F5 is all he needs—Brock Lesnar hoists Road Dogg onto his shoulders to finish him off with his signature finisher.

Breaking "The Brahma Bull"—not even The Rock can overcome John Cena's Attitude Adjustment.

Slam dunk—few Superstars can withstand the power of Mark Henry's World's Strongest Slam.

LaDDer MaYHeM

Superstars competing in Ladder Matches are supposed to climb up a ladder to claim a WWE title, a Money in the Bank briefcase, or some other valuable object. However, Superstars also use the ladders as jumping-off points for daring aerial moves—or as devastating weapons.

John Morrison creates a most extreme version of a moonsault, launching himself and a ladder onto multiple opponents.

Kofi Kingston prevents Seth Rollins from reaching the briefcase by back-body dropping him off the top of a ladder onto another ladder.

CM Punk's bid to weaponize a ladder by spinning it around is halted by a well-timed spear from Edge.

Roman Reigns uses a ladder to claim multiple victims, powerbombing Neville onto Kofi Kingston.

Jeff Hardy performs more daredevil aerial wizardry, leaping off a ladder down onto Edge, who is draped across a ladder.

"WHAT AN INNOVATIVE WAY TO USE THAT LADDER AS A WEAPON!"

JIM ROSS

Mankind slams a steel chair into a ladder, crushing the chest of The Rock.

The Rock's planned ladder attack fails when Triple H counters him with a steel chair.

THe SHieLD BReaKs!

Double crossed

In the first half of 2014, The Shield was on an impressive run of victories. After a dominant performance at *WrestleMania 30*, they found themselves in an extended rivalry with the villainous Evolution faction—Triple H, Batista, and Randy Orton. The Shield came out on top at *Payback*, but Evolution and Authority leader Triple H proclaimed on *RAW* the next night that he always had a Plan B. That plan turned out to be fracturing The Shield by convincing Seth Rollins to betray his friends and join The Authority. Rollins stunned Ambrose and Reigns by blasting them both with chair shots before aligning himself with Triple H and Randy Orton.

The trio known as The Shield—Dean Ambrose, Seth Rollins, and Roman Reigns—seemed unstoppable. Then Triple H made Seth Rollins an offer he couldn't refuse ...

Dean Ambrose writhes in agony from a chair shot so brutal that it bends the steel of the chair!

"YOU DON'T THINK I HAVE THE RIGHT TO DESTROY MY OWN CREATION?"

SETH ROLLINS

After a shocking attack on Roman Reigns, Seth Rollins puts Dean Ambrose down with a series of blows from a steel chair.

BETRAYED!

Rollins presents the dented chair to Randy Orton as a peace offering—and to show that Rollins has now aligned with The Authority.

Triple H gloats that he has the two faces of WWE—current championship contender Randy Orton and future champion Seth Rollins—under his sway.

WWE's WilDest

Spooky, clownish, mysterious, or just downright peculiar—over the years, some extremely unusual individuals and groups have called WWE home ...

Papa Shango tried to use his knowledge of voodoo to play sinister mind games on opponents, but his spells rarely worked!

Alarm call—WWE Superstars and fans are always unnerved when the bizarre, worm-eating Boogeyman makes an appearance.

Challenging perceptions of what was "normal," The Oddities tag team came in all shapes and sizes and were full of surprises!

Hornswoggle started as a leprechaunlike villain, but fans soon embraced his wild and goofy antics. He was once even thought to be Mr. McMahon's son!

Max Moon claimed to be from outer space, but his otherworldly talents didn't help him defeat Shawn Michaels on *RAW*'s first show.

Doink the Clown relished playing tricks on WWE Superstars. He also had a mini sidekick named Dink to help him cause extra confusion.

Looking to thrill fans with a look he based on a supervillain in an imaginary comic book, Cody Rhodes took the moniker Stardust.

Flamboyant, enigmatic, multititle winner Goldust unsettled opponents with his antics. Most WWE Superstars didn't know what to make of him, but they underestimated him at their peril!

"What's yours is mine!"—the Repo Man was always on the lookout for ways to "repossess" stuff and tangle rivals up with his tow rope.

TALKIN' TRASH

THE CHUMP WILL RUN, THE CHUMP WILL HIDE, AND I'LL HAVE TO CHASE HIM DOWN.

JESSE "THE BODY" VENTURA ABOUT HULK HOGAN

YOU'RE RIGHT ABOUT ONE THING, TRISH. I AM THE WALKING KISS OF DEATH. THIS SUNDAY, PUCKER UP!

LITA TO TRISH STRATUS

Daredevil moves and a bone-crushing finisher are just part of a Superstar's armory. A smart mouth is also useful, especially when setting a rival up for a fall.

THERE ARE THINGS YOU DON'T DO IN LIFE. YOU DON'T TUG ON SUPERMAN'S CAPE.

ROMAN REIGNS

YOU GONNA FIGHT ME? YOU GONNA PUNCH ME IN THE FACE? OR DO YOU HAVE TO GO ASK YOUR WIFE PERMISSION FIRST ...?

CM PUNK TO TRIPLE H

KNOW YOUR ROLE AND SHUT YOU MOUTH!

THE ROCK TO ANYONE THAT ANNOYS HIM

I'M EVERY WOMAN'S DREAM AND EVERY MAN'S NIGHTMARE!

RIC FLAIR

I HAVE MY RESERVATION IN THE EMERGENCY ROOM, AND I WENT TO THE TROUBLE OF MAKING ONE FOR YOU, UNDERTAKER!

MANKIND TO UNDERTAKER

TRIPLE H, YOU ARE STANDING IN THE MIDDLE OF MY YARD. YOU DON'T WANT TO BE HERE. BAD THINGS HAPPEN IN MY YARD.

UNDERTAKER TO TRIPLE H

I WILL NEVER FORGIVE YOUR MOTHER FOR GIVING BIRTH TO YOU!

MR. MCMAHON TO HIS SON SHANE

IT'S NOT THAT I HATE YOU. I LIKE YOU A BUNCH. BUT YOU HAVE THAT FACE THAT I WANT TO PUNCH!

PAIGE TO AJ LEE

NOBODY, ESPECIALLY VINCE MCMAHON, TELLS STONE COLD STEVE AUSTIN WHAT TO DO. AND THAT'S THE BOTTOM LINE!

STONE COLD STEVE AUSTIN

Senior Editor Alastair Dougall
Project Editor Pamela Afram
Proofreader Kayla Dugger
Senior Designer Nathan Martin
Designers Thelma-Jane Robb, Gary Hyde
Senior Pre-Production Producer Marc Staples
Senior Producer Mary Slater
Managing Editor Sarah Harland
Managing Art Editor Vicky Short
Art Director Lisa Lanzarini
Publisher Julie Ferris

Global Publishing Manager Steve Pantaleo
Vice President, Interactive Products Ed Kiang
Vice President, Consumer Products Sylvia Lee
Senior Vice President, Consumer Products Sarah Cummins
Vice President—Photography Bradley Smith
Photo department Josh Tottenham, Frank Vitucci,
Georgiana Dallas, Jamie Nelson, Melissa Halladay
**Senior Vice President, Assistant General Counsel—
Intellectual Property** Lauren Dienes-Middlen
Senior Vice President, Creative Services Stan Stanski
Creative Director John Jones
Project Manager Brent Mitchell

First American Edition, 2020
Published in the United States by DK Publishing
1450 Broadway, Suite 801, New York, NY 10018

Page design copyright © 2020 Dorling Kindersley Limited
DK, a Division of Penguin Random House LLC
20 21 22 23 24 10 9 8 7 6 5 4 3 2 1
001–316364–Mar/2020

A catalog record for this book is available
from the Library of Congress.
ISBN: 978-1-4654-8998-2

DK books are available at special discounts when purchased
in bulk for sales promotions, premiums, fund-raising, or
educational use. For details, contact:
DK Publishing Special Markets, 345 Hudson Street, New York,
New York 10014 SpecialSales@dk.com

Printed and bound in China

A WORLD OF IDEAS:
SEE ALL THERE IS TO KNOW

www.dk.com
www.wwe.com